THE
CYNIC'S
LEXICON

THE
CYNIC'S
LEXICON

Jonathon Green

St. Martin's Press
New York

Library of Congress Cataloging in Publication Data

Green, Jonathon.
    The cynic's lexicon.

    1. Quotations, English. I. Title.
PN6081.G638   1985   082   85-1691
ISBN 0-312-18055-1

First published in Great Britain by Routledge & Kegan Paul plc.

First U.S. Edition

10 9 8 7 6 5 4 3 2 1

For David Jenkins

THE
CYNIC'S
LEXICON

Introduction

Traditionally, the dictionary of quotations is a moral document.
Replete with wise saws, profundities and admirable guide-lines of
every variety, it stands like some avuncular mentor, solid upon one's
shelf, no matter what literary fripperies surround it. Good, if for nothing
else, as a guide to the more complex crosswords, it is a boon to those
who wish to impress, with both the breadth of their knowledge and
depth of their learning. It is a good book, almost bearing the symbolic
capital letters; culled from so much literature, it is the repository of
centuries of received wisdom.

This dictionary is not traditional. Within its pages repose, without
a doubt, the words of many men and women long dead, a good number
of whom have offered their mite to more established compilations, but
the majority of the words included here, both ancient and modern, reflect
an attitude and an approach to life that are not on the whole available
in regular editions.

The intention of *The Cynic's Lexicon* is unashamedly amoral. There
may indeed be all those saws, profundities and guide-lines that readers
of the 'good books' will expect, but the opinions they offer are, in this
compiler's view, somewhat more to the point. Here are no anodyne
solutions, no saccharine sidesteps, no simon-pure pictures of a world
that does not exist. Here life is just as nasty, brutish and short as Hobbes
would have it, and the precepts herein echo his vilifications and more.

This collection brings readers the traditional world turned
deliberately upside down. Cardinal virtues are duly mocked, deadly
sins fêted. Here is the least salubrious but quite possibly most pertinent
advice available for all those who need to cut their own swathe through
an inhospitable world. 'There is no "what should be",' remarked that
master of the philosophy, Lenny Bruce, 'there is only what is.' This
dictionary deals strictly with what is, however tasteless that may be.

The cynic, of course, is by no means a beloved figure, even in a
world that in its nature sneers at his mere art. To know the price of
everything and the value of nothing may be frustrating, but Oscar
Wilde of all people must have known what he was saying. As the
most quoted single person in these pages, Wilde was obviously strictly
mercenary. The justification for this collection of what critics may

term negative and destructive aphorisms, sentiments and general remarks may be seen all around. And if some may turn to Wilde for their condemnation, then as compiler, I prefer the almost equally popular Ambrose Bierce, whose *Devil's Dictionary* of seventy-five years ago may have in part inspired this successor. 'Cynic, *n*: a blackguard whose faulty vision sees things as they are, not as they ought to be.'

JONATHON GREEN

Thematic Index

ACQUAINTANCE: Bierce
ACT: Agate, Renard, Richardson. (*See also*: APPLAUSE, AUDIENCE, PLAY)
ACTOR/ACTRESS: Brando, Carson, J., Hammond, Mizner, A., and Herford, Mizner, W., Sanders, Wilding. (*See also*: PERFORMER)
ADOLESCENCE: Anonymous
ADULT: Aldiss, de Beauvoir
ADULTERY: Anonymous
ADVERTISING: Bromfield, Chandler, Howe, Leacock, Levine, Orwell, Shoaff, Turner, E. S.
ADVICE: de la Grange, Helps, Hockney, Johnson, La Rochefoucauld, Smith, H., Whitehorn, Wilde
ALCOHOL: Chandler, Friedenberg, Shaw
ALCOHOLIC: Thomas
ALIMONY: Baer, Crisp, Mailer, Mencken, Wodehouse
AMBITION: Bierce, Landor
AMERICA/AMERICANS: Dunne, Goodman, Lebowitz, Russell, Stevenson, A., Thompson, Vidal, Wilde
APPLAUSE: Bierce, Canetti, Colton, Mencken, Vo Dong Giang. (*See also*: POPULARITY)
ARCHITECTURE: Levin, Smith, N.B., Wright
ARISTOCRACY: Chesterton, Shaw
ART: Connolly, Jonson, Mencken, Mortimer, R., Wilde
ARTIST: Booker, Connolly, Ezrin, Hockney, Trilling, Waugh, E.
ARTISTIC: Chesterton
ARTS: Beecham
AUDIENCE: Barkley. (*See also*: ACT, ACTOR, APPLAUSE)
AUTHOR: Baring, Mizner, M., Montesquieu, O'Malley, Wodehouse. (*See also*: NOVELIST, WRITER)

BAD: Allen, W., Balzac, Busch, Gracian, de Madariaga, Miller, M., Reverdy, Vidal, Wilde. (*See also*: EVIL)
BATTLE: Bierce. (*See also*: VICTORY, WAR)
BEAUTIFUL: Brooks, L., Dryden, Goldoni, Gracian, Lebowitz, Parker, D.
BEAUTY: Anonymous, Bierce, Montherlant, Rowland, Saki, York
BELIEF: Bartz, Bierce, Chapelain, Fuller, Mencken, Russell, Sartre, Wilde. (*See also*: MORALITY, OPINION, PRINCIPLES, THEORY, THOUGHT)
BELIEVE: Anonymous, Balzac, Johnson, Lobel, Mencken, Montaigne, Parker, D., Pavese, Rousseau, Russell, Smith, H. A., Stone, Whitehorn
BIGAMY: Anonymous
BLACK: Alinsky, Lester
BORE: Beaton, Bernbach, Bierce, Churchill, Hoffenstein, Huxley, A., Kirk, La Rochefoucauld, Le Bon, Montesquieu, Peter, Pryce-Jones, Sanders, Whitehorn
BOY: Hubbard, Norman, Phelps, Rowland, Stevenson, A. (*See also*: Child, Childhood)
BRITAIN/the BRITISH: Bevan, Macaulay, Ustinov. (*See also*: ENGLAND/the ENGLISH)
BUSINESS: Allen, H., Chandler, Cummings, S., Daley, Johnson, Lois, Rice, Shaw, Steinbeck, Wrigley, Young

CALIFORNIA: Allen, F., Allen, W.
CELIBATE: Léautaud
CHARITY: Saki
CHASTITY: Chaucer, de Gourmont
CHILD: Angelou, Baldwin, de Beauvoir, Binstead, Bruce, Chamfort, Connolly, Darrow, Ehrlich, Laing, Lebowitz, Lodge, Mailer, Mencken, Mitford, Orton, Russell, Shaw, Strindberg, Szasz, Taine, Whitman, Wilde, Wylie. (*See also*: BOY, GIRL, PARENTS)
CHILDHOOD: Aldiss
CIVILISATION: Aldrich, Berne, Connolly, Knox, Magritte, Martin, Ortega y Gasset, Rogers, Rowland, Waugh, A., Whitehead
CLASS: Acton, Battie
COMMITTEE: Berle, Cocks, Harkness
COMPUTER: Gallois
CONFERENCE: Allen, F.
CONFESSIONS: Dewar
CONFIDANT: Bierce
CONSCIENCE: Chamfort, Chisholm, de Madariaga, Mencken, Reverdy, Russell, Scholl, Schulberg, Smith, L. P., Taylor, Wells, C., Wiener, Wilde
CONSERVATIVE: Bierce, Hubbard, E., Twain
COPS: Chandler. (*See also*: POLICE)
COUNTRY: Amin, Behan, Brooks, M., Chesterton, Goering, Ionesco, Johnson, Maistre, Mencken. (*See also*: LAND, NATION)
COURAGE: Smith, H.
COWARDICE: Addington, Camus, Hubbard, E., Voltaire, Wilde
CRIME: Baudelaire, Beaton, Bierce, Chandler, Cioran, Genet, Irving, Morley, Quételet, Rice, Seneca, Stirner, Wills
CRIMINAL: Bakunin, Burroughs
CRITIC: Balliett, Behan, Hoffman, Mizner, W., Pollock, Shaw, Tynan
CRITICISM: Beecham
CULTURE: Christgau, Vonnegut, Weil
CYNICISM: Bernbach, Bierce, Harris, Rowland

DEAD: Disraeli, Goncourt, Maeterlinck, Williams, T.
DEATH: Chase, Darden, Francis, Franklin, Graffiti, Hobbes, Johnson, Lebowitz, Maeterlinck, Muggeridge, Orwell, Pavese, Pope, Stalin, Vidal. (*See also*: DIE, DYING, SUICIDE)
DECENCY: Crisp, Saki
DEFEAT: de Beauvoir
DELUSION: Chapelain, Didion, Disraeli, Mencken
DEMOCRACY: Alvarez, Barnes, Barry, Bevan, Bukowski, Catlin, Chesterton, Coren, Emerson, de Flers, Goering, Hutchins, Huxley, A., Lippmann, Lowell, Mencken, Miller, H., Peter, Rogers, Russell, Shaw, 'The Third Man', Wilde, Wilson, W. (*See also*: ELECTION, VOTE)
DICTATOR: Masaryck. (*See also*: LEADER, RULER, TYRANT)
DICTATORSHIP: Bukowski
DIE: Amin, Barrymore, Lockridge, Mencken, Parker, D., Wilde, Wilkes. (*See also*: DEATH)
DIPLOMACY: Chou En Lai, Culbertson, Stalin
DIPLOMATS: Kraus, Lie, Stinnett, Ustinov
DISILLUSION: Wilde
DRAMATIST: Tynan
DRINKING: Benchley, Romanoff. (*See also*: ALCOHOL, ALCOHOLIC)
DRUNKS: Roosevelt
DUTY: Behan, Derby, Montherlant, Shaw, Washington, Wilde
DYING: Maugham. (*See also*: DEATH, DIE)

EDITOR: Stevenson, A. (*See also*: NEWSPAPERS)
EDUCATE: Chesterton, Laing
EDUCATION: Douglas, N., Halifax, Kettering, Lasch, Lebowitz, Mizner, W., Peter, Seeger, Ustinov, Wells, H. G.
ELECT: Nathan

ELECTION: Bismarck, Rousseau, Shaw. (*See also:* VOTE)
ELECTORATE: Aitkin, Goodman. (*See also:* DEMOCRACY, PEOPLE)
ENEMY: Anouilh, Bierce, Brougham, Connolly, Cornford, Crisp, d'Héricault, Heine, Lippmann, Lytton, Musset, Nietzsche, Nodier, O'Nolan, Vo Dong Giang, Wilde
ENGLAND/the ENGLISH: Agate, Connolly, Crisp, Douglas, A., Halsey, Mikes, Muggeridge, Parker, D., Rousseau, Shaw, Spaeth. (*See also:* BRITAIN/the BRITISH)
EQUALITARIANS: Muggeridge
EQUALITY: Bentham, Connolly, Ionesco, Lasch, Russell, Trilling. (*See also:* DEMOCRACY)
EVIL: Bierce, Broun, Eliot, T. S., Kempton, La Rochefoucauld, Mencken, Strindberg, Voltaire, West, M. (*See also:* BAD, WICKED)
EXCUSE: Aesop, Baker, Bierce
EXPERIENCE: Anonymous, Antrim, Boorstin, Erasmus, Fadiman, Herford and Clay, Hofstadter, Johnson, Jones, F. P., Maurois, Seeger, Shaw, Stern, Wilde
EXPERT: Bohr, Butler, D., 'Warren's Rule', Wilson, C. E., Wright

FAILURE: Algren, Bierce, Heller, J., Johnson, Marx, G.
FAITH: Anonymous, Mizner, W., Nietzsche
FAMILY: Amory, de Chazal, Greer, Mizner, A., and Herford, Strindberg, Wilde. (*See also:* BOY, CHILD, CHILDHOOD, GIRL, HOME, PARENTS, YOUTH)
FASHION: Johnson, Shaw
FATHER: Anonymous, Chesterfield, Russell, Wilde
FEMALE: Bierce. (*See also:* GIRL, WOMAN)
FICTION: Adams, F. P. (*See also:* NOVEL)
FIGHT: Adler
FOLLY: Cummings, S., Goldsmith, Rowland, Wilde
FOOL: Adams, F. P., Barbey d'Aurevilly, Benchley, Bierce, Binstead, Butler, S. (1), Butler, S. (2), Camus, Chapman, Delavigne, Fielding, 'First Law of Debate', Franklin, Léautaud, Macmillan, Mencken, Rabelais, Russell, Shaw, 'Shaw's System'
FRAUD: Curtis
FREEDOM: Bagehot, Boyd-Orr, Burke, Frost, Greene, Hoffer, Kristofferson, Laing, Landor, Nietzsche, Pitt, Platt, Rousseau, Sartre, Tsvetayeva
FREELANCE: Benchley
FREE SPEECH: Broun, Chandler
FRIEND: Bierce, Canning, Chesterton, Collins, Cornford, Darrow, d'Héricault, Douglas, N., La Bruyère, La Rochefoucauld, Lippmann, Lytton, Marx, G., Mencken, de Musset, Parker, D., Saki, Talleyrand, Welles, Wilde. (*See also:* NEIGHBOUR)
FRIENDSHIP: Balzac, Bierce, Goldsmith, Mencken, O'Malley, Stevenson, R. L., Thoreau, Wilde
FUTURE: Camus, Esar, Harris, Huxley, A., Orwell

GENEROSITY: McLaughlin, Wodehouse
GENIUS: Berenson, Bogart, Colton, Goncourt, Hope, McIndoe, Swift, Vidal, York. (*See also:* TALENT)
GENTLEMAN: Esar, King, Tiarks, Wilde
GIRL: Angelou, Anonymous, Bankhead, Brooks, L., Esar, Fitzgerald, Hubbard, K., Lamarr, Léautaud, Lebowitz, Miller, M., Nathan, Parker, D., Phelps, Rowland, Sagan, Tucker, 'Yiddish Proverb'. (*See also:* CHILD, CHILDHOOD, FEMALE, WOMAN, YOUTH)
GLORY: Flaubert. (*See also:* SUCCESS)
GOD: Amiel, Anonymous, Anouilh, Barbey d'Aurevilly, Baring, Butler, S. (2), Chamfort, Connolly, Dumas fils, Eliot, G., Graffiti, Inge, Lebowitz, Lec, Lee, Levin, McCoughey, Mencken, Nietzsche, O'Malley, Parker, D., Rostand, Spaeth, Steiger, Stendhal, Swift, Szasz, Valéry, Voltaire, Wilde
GOOD: Allen, W., Amory, Bankhead, Barrymore, Block, Busch, Creighton, Eliot, T. S., Frame, Goering, Gracian, Holmes, Kempton, La Rochefoucauld, Little, Longworth, Loos, Luce, Machiavelli, Mencken, Miller, M., 'Night After Night', Reverdy, Thatcher, Twain, Vidal, Wilde. (*See also:* VIRTUE)
GOVERNMENT: Acton, Berenson, Bierce, Bismarck, Burke, Chesterton, Dryden, Emerson, Fox, Friedman, M., Hubbard, E., Hume, Inge, Johnson, Julber, Kempton, Lippmann, Maistre, Paine, Penn, Plato, Proudhon, Reagan, Reston, Russell, Shaw, Siegfried, Snowden, Stone, Tawney, Thoreau, Truman, Vidal, Voltaire, Wilde

GRATITUDE: Alsop, Bennett, W. C.
GUILTY: Orwell

HAPPINESS: Binstead, Bourget, Carlyle, Connolly, Des Rieux, Hemingway, Johnson, Lebowitz, Mancroft, Mencken, Muggeridge, Nietzsche, Pope, Reed, R., Swift, Szasz, Wilde
HATRED: Adams, H. B., Byron, Chandler, Chapman, Emerson, Ionesco, Levant, Macaulay, Orwell, 'Private Worlds', Rowland, Shaw, Strachey, 'Suddenly Last Summer', Vidal
HERO: Bierce, Brecht, Claudel, Fitzgerald, Mencken, Mizner, W.
HEROISM: Ionesco
HISTORIAN: Butler, S. (2), Guedalla, Herodotus
HISTORY: Allen, W., Bierce, Broun, Carlyle, Cioran, Cocteau, Durrell, Eban, Genet, Guedalla, Hegel, Herzen, Huxley, A., Irving, Johnson, Koestler, Marx, K., Napoleon, Nehru, Orwell, Ponge, Powell, J. E., 'Private Eye', Queneau, 'Rude Pravo', Tolstoy, Vidal, Voltaire, Wells, H. G., Wilde. (*See also*: PAST)
HOLLYWOOD: Allen, F., Johnston, Loos, Mizner, W., Parker, D., Reed, R. (*See also*: CALIFORNIA)
HOME: Frost, R. (*See also*: FAMILY)
HONESTY: Johnson, Marx, G., Moyers, Nixon, Russell, Stoppard
HONOUR: Emerson, Fielding, Friedman, B. J., McLaughlin, Mencken, Thoreau
HUMAN: Allen, F., Anonymous, Bagehot, Baum, Bierce, Brecht, Brittain, Bukowski, Camus, Churchill, Crisp, Dunsany, Eliot, T. S., Gerrold, Goethe, Haskins, Hubbard, E., Hume, Irving, Jessel, Johnson, Leacock, Lippmann, Maugham, Mauriac, Mencken, Muggeridge, Pitt, Sanders, Sartre, Shaw, Slater, Turner, E. S., Ustinov, Voltaire, Waugh, A., Wells, H. G., Wilde
HUSBAND: Adams, J., Anonymous, Balzac, Bierce, Burke, L. J., Cooper, Dewar, 'Ladies' Home Journal', Lawrenson, Mencken, Montaigne, Rowland, Saki, Smith, S.
HYPOCRISY: Balzac, La Rochefoucauld, Maugham
HYPOCRITE: Ingersoll, Marquis, Wilde

IDEA: Asimov, Bagehot, Briggs, Mencken, Ortega y Gasset, Rowland, Wilde
IDEALS: Buckley, Camus, Ford, Galsworthy, Huxley, A., Ibsen, Kempton, Mencken, Nicolson, Russell, Scargill, Shaw, Smith, L. P. (*See also*: PRINCIPLES)
IDEAS: Bentley, Chamfort, Cioran, Cocks, Conrad, Galbraith, Mencken, Voltaire, Wilde. (*See also*: THOUGHT)
IDEOLOGY: Ionesco
IGNORANCE: Angelou, Bentham, Berenson, Halifax, Le Berquier, Lytton, McLaughlin, Wilde. (*See also:* STUPIDITY)
ILLUSION: Connolly, Kubrick, Voltaire
IMITATION: Allen, F., Baldwin, J., Eliot, T. S., Hoffer, Trilling, Voltaire
INDIVIDUAL: Alvarez
INJUSTICE: Lec
INNOCENCE: Arnoux, Didion, Holmes, McLaughlin, Orwell, Publius Syrus
INSINCERITY: Baum, Hill, Wilde
INTELLECTUAL: Aron, Auden, Wilde

JEALOUSY: Orwell, Wells, H. G.
JEW: Bruce, Kraus, Roth
JOURNALISM: Cockburn, Kelen, Kraus, Moyers, Tomalin, Wilde, Zappa. (*See also*: NEWSPAPERS)
JUDGES: Colton, Wodehouse
JUSTICE: Bruce, Camus, Chandler, de Chazal, France, Ionesco, La Rochefoucauld, Mencken. (*See also*: LAW, LAWYER)

LABOUR: Bierce
LAND: Brecht
LAW: Amin, Bentham, Chandler, Connolly, Cromwell, Culbertson, France, Giraudoux, Montesquieu, Solon, Stirner, Vidal, Voltaire, Wilde. (*See also*: JUDGES)
LAWYER: Anonymous, Bentham, Brougham, Colton, Docquier, Frost, R., Mencken. (*See also*: JUSTICE)

LEADER: Brecht, Broun, Chase, Cicero, Goering, Kempton, Loos, Schiller, Truman. (*See also*: DICTATOR, PRESIDENT, RULER, STATESMAN, TYRANT)
LEGISLATION: Funkhouser. (*See also*: LAW)
LIAR: Adams, F. P., Hemingway, Herford, Jerome, Jones, J., Stone. (*See also*: LIE, UNTRUE)
LIBERALISM: Baraka, Bierce, Bruce, Frost, R., Gregory, Nietzsche, Orwell, Player, Price, Trilling, Tynan
LIBERALITY: Addington
LIBERTY: Bagehot, Bierce, Des Rieux, Gibbon, Halifax, Hand, Montesquieu, Rogers, Shaw, Tournier
LIE: Bismarck, Brecht, Butler, S. (2), Cocteau, Durbin, Evans, H., Ibsen, Johnson, Kraus, Ministry of Information, Orwell, Parker, D., Pavese, Pobedonostsev, Proust, Shoaff, Stevenson, A., Stone, Thatcher, Wotton, Wyatt. (*See also*: LIAR, UNTRUE)
LIFE: Allen, W., Anouilh, Aymé, Baudelaire, Binstead, Boorstin, Butor, Cherbuliez, Cioran, Connolly, Crisp, Darling, Delaforest, Evans, B., Fadiman, Garratt and Kidd, Gauguin, Graffiti, Guitry, Hobbes, Huneker, Johnson, Kafka, Kempton, Lehrer, Lennon, Lodge, Miller, A., Muggeridge, Orwell, Parker, D., Rowland, Santayana, Sartre, Smith, L. P., Stern, Stoppard, Vidal, Voltaire, Wilde, Wilkes, Williams, T.
LITERATURE: Wilder, T. (*See also*: NOVELS, WRITING)
LIVE: Brecht, Busch, Dumas fils, Francis, Franklin, Magritte, Mencken, Parker, D., Publius Syrus, Saki, Voltaire, Wilde
LIVES: Darrow, Reverdy, Wilde
LIVING: Anonymous, Barrymore, Cummings, E. E., Galbraith, Maeterlinck, Muggeridge, Pavese, Schulberg
LOVE: Allen, W., Anonymous, Anouilh, Atkinson, T.-G., Auden, Baudelaire, Beaumont and Fletcher, Beckett, Bierce, Blessington, Brecht, Brenan, Bruce, Bukowski, Byron, Capus, Chamfort, Chandler, Chesterfield, Coleman, Connolly, Crane, Diderot, Disraeli, France, 'French Proverb', Freud, Gabor, Goethe, Goldsmith, Greer, Halsey, Haskins, Hecht, Hemingway, Herford and Clay, Huxley, A., Julber, La Rochefoucauld, Laing, Lawrenson, Léautaud, Lee, Mailer, Maugham, Mauriac, Mencken, Mizner, W., Montagu, Nietzsche, Norman, Parker, D., Paternoster, 'Private Worlds', de Régnier, Rowland, Sagan, Sandberg, Shaw, Suckling, 'Suddenly Last Summer', Taine, Theophrastus, Tolstoy, Vidal, Wilde, Zangwill
LOVER: Anonymous, Bierce, Congreve, Connolly, Cooper, La Rochefoucauld, Lawrenson, Maugham, Parker, D., Rowland
LYING: Cornford, Evans, B., Lin Yutang, Lippmann, Parker, D. (*See also*: UNTRUE)

MALE: Bierce
MAN: Adams, A., Albee, Allen, W., Anonymous, Anouilh, Auden, Bacon, Balzac, Baring, Benson, Bossuet, Brecht, Butler, S. (1), Butler, S. (2), Camus, Chase, Chesterfield, Chevalier, Churchill, Clark, Colette, Congreve, Darling, Darlington, Disraeli, Esar, Fadiman, Francis, Gabor, Genet, Gibbs, G., Greer, Gyp, Herford and Clay, Hobbes, Hölderlin, Huxley, T. H., Inge, Jackson, Johnson, Kempton, Kingsmill, Koestler, Laing, Little, Mabley, Mailer, Malraux, Mancroft, Mencken, Napoleon, Nathan, Nietzsche, O'Nolan, Orwell, Pagnol, Parker, D., Reade, Rostand, Rousseau, Rowland, Russell, Sartre, Schweitzer, Skinner, Steiger, Thurber, Tournier, Turner, L., Twain, Valéry, Voltaire, Wallace, West, M., Wilde. (*See also*: MEN)
MANHOOD: Disraeli
MANKIND: Allen, W., Butler, S. (1), Camus, Darlington, Hobbes, Johnson, Kingsmill, Nietzsche, Russell, Smith, L.P., Voltaire
MANNERS: Balzac, Waugh, E.
MARKET: Anacharsis, Brecht
MARRIAGE: Amory, Anonymous, Bacon, Balzac, Baum, Beaumanoir, Benson, Bierce, Binstead, Butler, S. (2), Capus, Chekhov, Congreve, Connolly, Crisp, Diogenes, Des Rieux, Disraeli, Dreikurs, Dunn, Durbin, Fielding, Gabor, Gibbs, Goethe, Gyp, Herford and Clay, Howe, Hubbard, K., Johnson, Kipling, Lawrenson, Léautaud, Levant, Mailer, Maugham, Mizner, W., Montagu, Montaigne, Nathan, Pavese, Pryce-Jones, Rogers, S., Rowland, Shaw, Voltaire, Wilde. (*See also*: HUSBAND, WIFE, WEDDING)
MEDIA: Alvarez, Funkhouser, Goodman, Riesman. (*See also*: NEWSPAPERS, TELEVISION)
MEDICINE: Anonymous, Voltaire

MEDIOCRITY: Chamfort, Connolly, Heller, J., Lois, Mead, Montesquieu, Préault
MEN: Addison, Anonymous, 'The Bad and the Beautiful', Beaumanoir, Brooks, M., Chincholles, Cioran, Des Rieux, Diderot, Dumas fils, Eban, Eliot, T. S., Fadiman, Feiffer, Heller, J., Hitler, Hubbard, K., Huxley, A., de Madariaga, Mansfield, Maugham, Mead, Mencken, Morgan, Muggeridge, Nathan, Parker, D., Pavese, Pinero, Rosten, de Sévigné, Voltaire, Whitton, Wilde. (*See also*: MALE, MAN)
MODESTY: Herford, Reverdy
MONEY: Adams, J., Auden, Baraka, Baring, Brenan, Chandler, Ciardi, Cicero, Connolly, Crisp, Donleavy, Francis, Guitry, Hurley, Johnson, Leacock, Luce, O'Nolan, Paternoster, Pavese, de Régnier, Thatcher, Turner, L., Voltaire, Wilde
MORAL: Binstead, De Sica, Ferber, Lester, Mencken, de Sade, Strachey, Tolstoy, Wells, H. G., Wilde, Wyatt
MORALIST: Canetti, Russell, Salm-Dyck, Wilde
MORALITY: Alvarez, Bolt, Johnson, Macaulay, Nietzsche, Russell, Shaw, Twain, Whitehead, Wilde
MORALS: Baker, Brecht
MURDER: Koestler, Rostand, Shaw, Wilde
MUSIC: Beecham
MYTH: Bierce, Brogan, Camus, Cooper, Feibleman, Greer, Heller, R., Sartre, Whitman, Wilde

NATION: Amin, Balzac, Cioran, Eban, Kubrick, Mencken, Pompidou, Strachey. (*See also*: COUNTRY, LAND, STATE)
NATURE: Clark, Darden, Friedenberg, Inge, Jackson, Lebowitz, Lockridge, Phelps, Reverdy, Rowland, Russell, Vidal, Voltaire
NEIGHBOUR: Ade, Aretino, Bradley, Franklin, Lec, Lie, Truman. (*See also*: ACQUAINTANCE, FRIEND, OTHERS)
NEWS: Brecht, Stone
NEWSPAPERS: Allen, F., Bevan, Chandler, King, Knoll, Simonds. (*See also*: JOURNALISM, MEDIA, PRESS)
NOVELIST: Auden, Connolly, Cooper. (*See also*: AUTHOR, WRITER)
NOVELS: Adams, F. P., Wodehouse

OBSCENITY: Anonymous, Russell. (*See also*: PORNOGRAPHY)
OLD: Chapman, Diogenes, Disraeli, Franklin, La Rochefoucauld, Leacock, Macmillan, Maugham, O'Malley, Saki, Salm-Dyck, Sayers, Smith, L. P., Swift, Wilde
OPERA: Amory
OPINION: About, Cicero, Crisp, Disraeli, Halifax, Lichtenberg, Lytton, Maugham, Oliver, Pagnol, Platt, Russell, Taylor, Wilde
OPTIMISM: Anonymous, Cabell, Fitzgerald, Hubbard, E., Kraus, Oppenheimer, Ustinov
OTHER: Baker, Balzac, Caesar, Chesterfield, Compton-Burnett, Crisp, Guedalla, Hoffer, La Rochefoucauld, Lowell, Sartre, Shaw, Terry-Thomas, Truman, Twain, Wilde, Williams, T., Wolf
OTHERS: Connolly, Dumas père, Eban, Guitry, Gyp, Halifax, Hazlitt, Hobbes, Johnson, Karr, Kirk, Maugham, Mencken, Nicolson, Nietzsche, Ophuls, Petit, Taylor, Voltaire, Wilde. (*See also*: NEIGHBOUR)

PARANOID: Burroughs
PARENTS: Darrow, Laing, Lebowitz, Peter, Roth, Strindberg, Tucker. (*See also*: BOY, CHILD, GIRL)
PARTY: Bierce, Chesterton, Disraeli, Dwight, Emerson, Halifax, La Bruyère, Mencken, Nietzsche, Pope, Stone, Swift. (*See also*: POLITICS)
PAST: Connolly, Esar, Halifax, Wolf. (*See also*: HISTORY)
PATRIOTISM: Chesterton, Conkling, Goering, Johnson, Léautaud, Mencken, Nathan, Shaw, Strachey, Twain, Wilde. (*See also*: COUNTRY, LAND)
PEACE: Bierce, Brecht, Chesterfield, Hitler, Lebowitz, Lippmann, Mauldin, Stone, 'The Third Man'
PEOPLE: Adams, F. P., Arlen, Bagehot, Baker, Barnes, Benchley, Bismarck, Boyd-Orr, Burke, E., Burnett, Burns, Carlyle, Chase, Claudel, Cioran, Creighton, Cromwell, Dunne, Ezrin, de Flers, Francis, Friedenberg, Friedman, M., Genet, Goering, Halifax, Hegel, Kraus, Lebowitz, Levine, Lincoln, Maugham, McCarthy, E., Mencken,

Mizner, W., Mortimer, Penn, Peter, Platt, Riesman, Röhm, Rudin, Sellers, Siegfried, Slater, Vidal, Voltaire, Wilde

PERFORMER: Bruce. (*See also*: ACTOR)

PESSIMISM: Broun, Cabell, Hubbard, E., Nietzsche, Oppenheimer, Shaw, Triolet, Ustinov

PHILANTHROPY: Wilde

PHILOSOPHY: Goldsmith, Graffiti, Harris, Kempton, Marquis, Voltaire

PLAGIARISM: Inge, Mizner, W., Parker, D.

PLAY: Tynan. (*See also:* ACT, DRAMATIST)

POET: Auden

POLICE: Burroughs, Stevenson, R. L. (*See also*: COPS)

POLITICIAN: Adams, F. P., Aitkin, Baker, Barnes, Bellow, Cameron, Chambers, De Gaulle, Dwight, Francis, Galsworthy, Kelen, Kent, Khrushchev, Lippmann, Lloyd George, Mencken, Milligan, Moyers, Nietzsche, Oliver, Pompidou, Reed, T. B., Russell, Simonds, Truman, Wyatt. (*See also*: STATESMAN)

POLITICS: Adams, F. P., Adams, H. B., Baker, Bierce, Brittain, Camus, Chandler, Chesterton, Churchill, Cicero, Culbertson, Disraeli, Galbraith, Goethe, Graffiti, Huxley, A., Johnson, Lester, McCarthy, Mencken, Nathan, Proust, Rakove, Reston, Riesman, Roche, Valéry, Vidal, Wolfe. (*See also*: GOVERNMENT, PARTY)

POOR: Bacon, Bierce, Billings, Brenan, Chamfort, France, Hancock, Herold, Janet, Rabelais, Sartre, Trilling

POPULARITY: Mencken. (*See also*: APPLAUSE)

PORNOGRAPHY: Tynan, White, Ed. (*See also*: OBSCENITY)

POWER: Adams, A., Anouilh, Baker, Culbertson, Galsworthy, Goering, Hand, Hobbes, Huxley, A., Jones, W., Lippmann, Nietzsche, Orwell, Snowden, Tooke, Tsvetayeva, Wolfe. (*See also*: GOVERNMENT)

PRESIDENT: Baker, Bellow, Broder, Brooks, M., Darrow, Jellinek, Stevenson, A., Wilde. (*See also*: LEADER, RULER)

PRESS: Chandler, Nixon. (*See also*: JOURNALISM, NEWSPAPERS)

PRINCIPLES: Addington, Adler, Barzun, Bentley, E., Bierce, Bismarck, Huxley, A., Jones, E., Lloyd George, McKinley, Maugham, Nathan, Pritchett, Rakove, de Sade, Shaw, Steiger. (*See also*: BELIEF, IDEALS, MORAL, OPINION, THOUGHT)

PROFESSION: Saki

PROGRESS: Bagehot, Baker, Butler, S. (2), Dunsany, Ellis, Lec, Trilling. (*See also:* SCIENCE)

PROPAGANDA: Chandler, Cornford, Eban, Hitler, Lippmann, 'Saturday Night and Sunday Morning'

PSYCHIATRY: Adams, J., Peter

PSYCHO-ANALYSIS: Kraus, Mencken

PUBLIC: Acheson, Asimov, Burke, E., Carlyle, Chamfort, Disraeli, Johnson, Loos, Macaulay, Penrose, Platt, Russell, Shaw, Skelton, Wilde

PURITANISM: Mencken, Ophuls

RACIAL: Alinsky

REALITY: Berlin, Broun, Buckley, Harris, McCarthy, M.

REBEL: Bierce. (*See also*: REVOLUTION)

REFORM: Conkling, Hazlitt, Lippmann, Smith, L. P., Twain, Walker

RELATIONS: Wilde. (*See also*: FAMILY)

RELIGION: Ellis, Feibleman, Ionesco, Mencken, Nietzsche, Saki, Steiger, Stendhal, Strachey, Ustinov, Whitman, Wilde, Wolfe

REMORSE: Mencken

RESPECT: Mencken

REVENGE: Anonymous, Beard, Beaumanoir, Bossuet, Gauguin, Guitry, Le Bon, Vapereau.

REVOLUTION: Berrigan, Bierce, Burke, E., Camus, Conrad, Douglas, A., Kafka, Kempton, Ortega y Gasset, Santayana, Shaw

RICH: Anouilh, Baraka, Bierce, Billings, Brown, Céline, Chamfort, Ciardi, Connolly, France, Grigg, Helps, Leonard, Marquis, Wilde

RIGHT: Chesterfield, Hazlitt, Huxley, A., Moore, Szasz, Voltaire, Waugh, E., Wilde

ROBBERY: Brecht, Mencken, Twain. (*See also*: STEAL, THIEF)

RULER: Bierce, Hitler, Kraus, Mencken, Vidal. (*See also*: DICTATOR, GOVERNMENT, LEADER, POWER, TYRANT)

SATIRE: Kaufman, Swift
SCIENCE: Anonymous, Baker, Butler, S. (2), Cummings, E. E., Koestler, Wilde. (*See also*: PROGRESS)
SCIENTIST: Asimov, Clarke, 'Mann's Law'
SELF-RESPECT: Mencken
SENTIMENT: Wilde
SEX: Allen, W., Anonymous, Barrymore, Bukowski, Chandler, Francis, Lodge, Lownes, Maugham, Mikes, Vidal, White, Ed.
SHAME: Sandberg
SIN: Arnoux, Beckett, Feiffer, France, Lebowitz, Little, de Madariaga, Mencken, Morley, Rowland, Saki, Stocks
SINCERITY: Crisp, Maugham, Stalin
SOCIAL: Amory, Thoreau, Williams, K.
SOCIETY: Aldiss, Chamfort, Chincholles, Frost, Goodman, Laing, Lin Yutang, McLaughlin, Martin, Maugham, Paine, Quételet, Rousseau, Shaw, Stone
SON: Anonymous, Chesterfield. (*See also*: BOY, CHILD)
SPEECH: Broun, Goodman, Rogers
SPORT: Orwell
STATE: Bakunin, Grigg, Hegel, Hölderlin, Richelieu, Stirner. (*See also:* NATION)
STATESMAN: Acheson, Bierce, Connally, Friedman, M., Hubbard, K., Lloyd George, Pompidou, Reed, T. B., Truman, Twain. (*See also*: POLITICIAN)
STEAL: Eliot, T. S., Trilling. (*See also*; ROBBERY, THIEF)
STRENGTH: Bidault, Runyon, Ustinov, Voltaire, Wilde
STUPIDITY: Bagehot, Demartini. (*See also*: IGNORANCE)
SUCCESS: Canetti, Chamfort, Cocteau, Eliot, T. S., 'Glyme's Formula', Heller, J., Heller, R., Lasch, Lebowitz, Lippmann, Maugham, Nathan, O'Malley, Pendred, Reed, T. B., Seneca, Solomons, Tomalin, Turner, L., Voltaire, Wyatt. (*See also*: GLORY)
SUICIDE: Baechler. (*See also*: DEATH)

TACT: Cocteau, Mortimer
TALENT: Agate, Angelou, Booker, Connolly, De Bono, France, Goncourt, Vidal. (*See also*: GENIUS)
TEENAGER: Lebowitz
TELEVISION: Allen, F., Allen, W., Anonymous, Barnes, Carson, R., Coren, Crisp, Frost, D., Galbraith, Kovacs, Lebowitz, Levinson, Nixon, Sarraute. (*See also*: MEDIA)
THEORY: Koestler, 'Mann's Law', Marquis, Mencken, 'Murphy's Law of Research', Parker, R. B., Yates. (*See also*: BELIEF, OPINION, PRINCIPLES, THOUGHT)
THIEF: Bierce, Chesterton, Ingersoll, O'Malley. (*See also*: ROBBERY, STEAL)
THOUGHT: Adams, F. P., Amiel, Anouilh, Balzac, Baring, Bidault, Brenan, Burbank, Burke, E., Chapman, Coren, Emerson, Fadiman, Fuller, Hitler, Ionesco, James, Johnson, Jones, B., Karr, Lebowitz, Lin Yutang, Lippmann, Loos, 'Matz's Maxim', Oppenheimer, Penn, Pope, Reade, Rostand, Russell, Santayana, Shaw, Siegfried, Talleyrand, Ustinov, Veeck, Vidal, Wilde, Wright
TIME: Berlioz, Bruce, 'Chinese Curse', Crisp, Delaforest, Friedenberg, Garratt and Kidd, Johnson, Levant, Muggeridge
TOOLS: Nietzsche
TRADITION: Demartini
TRUTH: Aretino, Baldwin, S., Balfour, Butler, S. (2), Disraeli, Eldridge, Faulkner, Giraudoux, Guedalla, Herford, Hitler, Jenkins, Jerome, Johnson, Knoll, Lippmann, Mencken, Ministry of Information, Orwell, Sartre, Shoaff, Smith, L. P., Stone, Summerskill, Voltaire, Whitehead, Wilde
TYRANT: Aesop, Bierce, Cioran, Johnson, Miller, H., Pitt, Platt, Russell, Shaw, Strindberg, Wilde. (*See also:* DICTATOR, LEADER, RULER)

UNEDUCATED: Wilde. (*See also:* IGNORANCE, STUPIDITY)
UNHAPPINESS: Brecht, Chase, De Bono, Marx, G., Mencken
UNTRUE: Anonymous, Mencken. (*See also*: LIAR, LIE)

VANITY: Johnson, La Rochefoucauld
VICE: Dunne, Johnson, La Rochefoucauld, Maugham
VICTIM: About

VICTORY: de Beauvoir (*See also*: BATTLE, WAR)
VIOLENCE: Friedenberg, Laing, O'Brien, Orwell, Stirner
VIRTUE; Angelou, Anonymous, Bevan, Bierce, Binstead, France, Johnson, Karr, La Rochefoucauld, Le Bon, Lewis, Lippmann, Proudhon, Seneca, Shaw, Skinner, Stekhel, Strindberg, Swift, Thoreau, Veeck, Wilde. (*See also*: GOOD)
VOTE: Adams, F. P., Bukowski, Fields, Levin, Nathan. (*See also*: DEMOCRACY, ELECTION)

WAR: Anonymous, Bennett, A., Bismarck, Brecht, Brooks, M., Chou En Lai, Churchill, Clemenceau, Erasmus, Goering, Hitler, Kraus, Lippmann, Montaigne, Orwell, Powell, J. E., Rogers, Russell, Schlesinger, Stone, Tuchman, Wilde, Wills. (*See also*: BATTLE, VICTORY)
WEAK: Bidault, Ustinov, Voltaire, Wilde
WEDDING: Bierce, Heine, Herford and Clay. (*See also*: MARRIAGE)
WHITE: Alinsky, Lester, Powell, A. C.
WICKED: Wilde. (*See also*: BAD, EVIL)
WIFE: Adams, J., Albee, Anonymous, Auden, Brooks, M., Bruce, Burke, L. J., Campbell, Chamfort, Chesterfield, Connolly, Cooper, Cummings, E. E., Darling, Dryden, Friedman, B. J., Gay, Guitry, Hicks, Johnson, 'Ladies' Home Journal', Luce, Mancroft, Maugham, Mencken, Montaigne, Parker, D., Rostand, Rowland. (*See also*: MARRIAGE)
WOMAN: Addison, Algren, Anonymous, Atkinson, T.-G., Balzac, Barbey d'Aurevilly, Beaumanoir, Beerbohm, Benson, Bierce, Binstead, Bossuet, Butler, S. (2), Byron, Capus, Connolly, Dewar, Diderot, Disraeli, Eliot, G., Feiffer, Ferber, Fields, Francis, Gibbs, G., Giraudoux, Gracian, Gyp, Herford and Clay, Jenkins, Juvenal, King, Kraus, La Rochefoucauld, Lawrenson, Lebowitz, Luce, Mabley, Mailer, Maugham, Mead, Mencken, Millett, Montagu, Morgan, Nathan, Norman, Ovid, Pavese, Rowland, Saki, Sandberg, Scott, Shaw, Skinner, Strindberg, Tolstoy, Tournier, Turner, L., Vapereau, Wallace, Whitton, Wilde. (*See also*: FEMALE, GIRL)
WORK: Drucker, Francis, Hockney, Peter, Romanoff, Rowland, Voltaire
WORLD: Allen, W., Balfour, Balzac, Beard, Butler, S. (1), Cabell, Ellis, Franklin, Hitler, Leopardi, Lloyd George, McCarthy, Magritte, Mencken, Nietzsche, Oppenheimer, Parker, D., Santayana, Swift, Twain, Ustinov, Voltaire, Zappa
WRITER: Camus, Connolly, Crisp, De Vries, Didion, Faulkner, Francis, Kraus, Lennon and McCartney, Mencken, West, R. (*See also*: AUTHOR, NOVELIST)
WRITING: Condon, Donleavy, Johnson, Mailer, Marquis, Orwell, Steinbeck
WRONG: Chesterfield, Griswold, Hazlitt, Huxley, A., 'Jones' Law', Krutch, Moore, Rutherford, Saki, Szasz, Voltaire, Waugh, E., Wilde

YOUTH: Bacon, Bagehot, Barrymore, Beerbohm, Binstead, Chapman, Connolly, Crisp, Diogenes, Disraeli, Fuldheim, Herford and Clay, Hitler, Hurley, Kipling, Macmillan, Maugham, Orwell, Saki, Smith, L. P., Whitehorn, Wilde

EDMOND ABOUT
1828–1885　French political writer

It has long been noticed that juries are pitiless for robbery and full of indulgence for infanticide. A question of interest, my dear Sir! The jury is afraid of being robbed and has passed the age when it could be a victim of infanticide.

> quoted in *A Cynic's Breviary* by J. R. Solly, 1925

Marriage, in life, is like a duel in the midst of a battle.

DEAN ACHESON
1893–1971　American government official

on leaving his post as Secretary of State, 1952:

I will undoubtedly have to seek what is happily known as gainful employment, which I am glad to say does not describe holding public office

A memorandum is written not to inform the reader but to protect the writer.

The first requirement of a statesman is that he be dull. This is not always easy to achieve.

> 1970

LORD ACTON
1834–1902　British statesman

The danger is not that a particular class is unfit to govern. Every class is unfit to govern.

> letter to Mary Gladstone, 1881

ABIGAIL ADAMS
1744–1818   American letter writer

I am more and more convinced that man is a dangerous creature and that power, whether vested in many or a few, is ever grasping, and like the grave, cries 'Give, give.'

quoted 1775

FRANKLIN P. ADAMS (F.P.A.)
1881–1960   American journalist

The trouble with this country is that there are too many politicians who believe, with a conviction based on experience, that you can fool all of the people all of the time.

Nods and Becks, 1944

When a man you like switches from what he said a year ago, or four years ago, he is a broad-minded person who has courage enough to change his mind with changing conditions. When a man you don't like does it, he is a liar who has broken his promises.

Ibid.

When the political columnists say 'Every thinking man' they mean themselves; and when the candidates appeal to 'every intelligent voter', they mean everybody who is going to vote for them.

Ibid.

The best part of the fiction in many novels is the notice that the characters are purely imaginary.

HENRY BROOKS ADAMS
1838–1918   American historian

Politics, as a practice, whatever its professions, has always been the systematic organisation of hatreds.

The Education of Henry Adams, 1907

Practical politics consists in ignoring facts.

Ibid.

JOEY ADAMS
1911– American comedian

The most popular labor-saving device today is still a husband with money.

Cindy and I, 1959

A psychiatrist is a fellow who asks you a lot of expensive questions your wife asks you for nothing.

Ibid.

HENRY ADDINGTON, Viscount Sidmouth
1757–1844 British Prime Minister

I hate liberality – nine times out of ten it is cowardice, and the tenth time lack of principle.

JOSEPH ADDISON
1672–1719 British poet and statesman

Men who cherish for women the highest respect are seldom popular with them.

GEORGE ADE
1866–1944 American humorist

If it were not for the presents, an elopement would be preferable.

Forty Modern Fables, 1901

Do unto yourself as your neighbours do unto themselves and look pleasant.

Hand Made Fables, 1920

ALFRED ADLER
1870–1937 German psychoanalyst

It is easier to fight for one's principles than to live up to them.

quoted in *Alfred Adler* by P. Bottome, 1939

3

AESOP
fl. 6th century BC   Greek fabulist

Any excuse will serve a tyrant.

Fables

JAMES AGATE
1877–1947   British film and drama critic

The English instinctively admire any man who has no talent and is modest about it.

Theatre director: a person engaged by the management to conceal the fact that the players cannot act.

DON AITKIN
1937–   Australian politician

Whatever politicians, activists and manipulators propose, it is the phlegmatic, indifferent, ingrained electorate which disposes.

quoted 1969

EDWARD ALBEE
1928–   American playwright

The way to a man's heart is through his wife's belly, and don't you forget it.

Who's Afraid of Virginia Woolf?, 1964

BRIAN ALDISS
1925–   British science fiction writer

When childhood dies, its corpses are called adults and they enter society, one of the politer names of hell. That is why we dread children, even if we love them. They show us the state of our decay.

Guardian, 1971

THOMAS B. ALDRICH
1836–1907   American poet and editor

Civilisation is the lamb's skin in which barbarism masquerades.
Ponkapog Papers, 1903

ALEXANDER II
1818–1881   Russian monarch

It is better to abolish serfdom from above than to wait for it to abolish itself from below.

1856

NELSON ALGREN
1909–1981   American writer

Never eat at a place called Mom's. Never play cards with a man named Doc. And never lie down with a woman who's got more troubles than you.
What Every Young Man Should Know

The avocation of assessing the failures of better men can be turned into a comfortable livelihood, providing you back it up with a Ph.D.
Writers at Work, 1st series, 1958

SAUL ALINSKY
1909–1972   American radical

A racially integrated community is a chronological term timed from the entrance of the first black family to the exit of the last white family.

FRED ALLEN (John F. Sullivan)
1894–1956   American humorist

Hollywood is a place where people from Iowa mistake each other for a star.

Hollywood is a great place if you're an orange.

also cited as –

California is a fine place to live in – if you're an orange.

A conference is a gathering of important people who singly can do nothing but together can decide that nothing can be done.

To a newspaper man a human being is an item with skin wrapped around it.

Imitation is the sincerest form of television.

quoted in Esquire magazine, 1971

HUBERT ALLEN
b. 1872   American financier

Look, we trade every day out there with hustlers, deal-makers, shysters, con-men. That's the way businesses get started. That's the way this country was built.

WOODY ALLEN (Allen Konigsberg)
1935–   American film director and screenwriter

Love is the answer, but while you are waiting for the answer, sex raises some pretty good questions.

New York Herald Tribune, 1975

Life is a concentration camp. You're stuck here and there's no way out and you can only rage impotently against your persecutors.

Esquire magazine, 1977

Is sex dirty? Only if it's done right.

All You Ever Wanted to Know about Sex, 1972

In California they don't throw their garbage away – they make it into television shows.

Annie Hall, 1977

Life is divided into the horrible and the miserable.

Ibid.

It seemed the world was divided into good and bad people. The good ones slept better ... while the bad ones seemed to enjoy the waking hours much more.

Side Effects, 1981

More than any other time in history, mankind faces a crossroads. One path leads to despair and utter hopelessness. The other, to total extinction. Let us pray we have the wisdom to choose correctly.

Ibid.

Don't knock masturbation – it's sex with someone I love.

JOSEPH ALSOP
1910– American political journalist

Gratitude, like love, is never a dependable international emotion.

Observer, 1952

ROBERT ALTMAN
1922– American film director

What's a cult? It just means not enough people to make a minority.

Observer, 1981

AL ALVAREZ
1929– British writer and poet

Mass democracy, mass morality and the mass media thrive independently of the individual, who joins them at a cost of at least a partial perversion of his instinct and insights. He pays for his social ease with what used to be called his soul, his discriminations, his uniqueness, his psychic energy, his self.

The Listener, 1971

HENRI FRÉDÉRIC AMIEL
1821–1881 French writer

Tell me what you think you are and I will tell you what you are not.

Journal intime, 1866

We are always making God our accomplice so that we may legalise our own iniquities. Every successful massacre is consecrated by a Te Deum, and the clergy have never been wanting in benedictions for any victorious enormity.

Ibid.

IDI AMIN DADA
1935–   Ugandan dictator

In any country there must be people who have to die. They are the
sacrifices any nation has to make to achieve law and order.

quoted 1976

KINGSLEY AMIS
1922–   British author

More will mean worse.

Encounter magazine, 1960

CLEVELAND AMORY
1907–   American writer

The opera is like a husband with a foreign title – expensive to support,
hard to understand and therefore a supreme social challenge.

on NBC-TV, 1961

Relations between the sexes are so complicated that the only way
you can tell if two members of the set are 'going together' is if they
are married. Then, almost certainly, they are not.

Who Killed Society?, 1960

A 'good' family is one that used to be better.

Ibid.

ANACHARSIS
fl. 6th century BC   Greek philosopher

A market is a place set apart for men to deceive and get the better of
one another.

quoted in *Lives and Opinions of Eminent Philosophers*
by Diogenes Laertius

MAYA ANGELOU
1928–   American writer

Most plain girls are virtuous because of the scarcity of opportunity to
be otherwise.

I Know Why the Caged Bird Sings, 1969

Children's talent to endure stems from their ignorance of alternatives.

Ibid.

JEAN ANOUILH
1910–   French playwright

Oh, love is real enough, you will find it some day, but it has one arch-enemy – and that is life.

Ardèle, 1948

Every man thinks God is on his side. The rich and powerful know that he is.

The Lark, 1955

MINNA ANTRIM
b. 1861   American writer

Experience is a good teacher, but she sends in terrific bills.

Naked Truth and Veiled Allusions, 1902

PIETRO ARETINO
1492–1556   Italian satirist

If you want to annoy your neighbours, tell the truth about them.

MICHAEL ARLEN (Dikran Kuyumjian)
1895–1956   Armenian-born British novelist

It's amazing how nice people are to you when they know you're going away.

ALEXANDRE ARNOUX
1894–1973   French writer

The state of innocence contains the germs of all future sin.

Études et caprices

RAYMOND ARON
1905–1983   French political thinker

What passes for optimism is most often the effect of an intellectual error.

The Opium of the Intellectuals, 1957

ISAAC ASIMOV
1920–   American science fiction writer

When the lay public rallies round to an idea that is denounced by distinguished but elderly scientists and supports that idea with great fervour and emotion, the distinguished but elderly scientists are then, after all, right.

Fantasy and Science Fiction magazine, 1977

BROOKS ATKINSON
1894–1984   American critic

There is a good deal of solemn cant about the common interests of capital and labour. As matters stand, their only common interest is that of cutting each other's throat.

Once Around the Sun, 1951

TI-GRACE ATKINSON
1938–   American feminist

The vast majority of women who pretend vaginal orgasms are faking it to 'get the job'.

Love is the victim's response to the rapist.

W. H. AUDEN
1907–1973   British poet

No poet or novelist wishes he was the only one who ever lived, but most of them wish they were the only one alive, and quite a number fondly believe their wish has been granted.

The Dyer's Hand, 1962

Money cannot buy
The fuel of love
but is excellent kindling.

To the man-in-the-street, who, I'm sorry to say,
Is a keen observer of life,
The word intellectual suggests right away
A man who's untrue to his wife.

from Collected Shorter Poems 1927–1957, 1966

MARCEL AYMÉ
1902–1967   French writer

Life always comes to a bad end.

Les Oiseaux de lune, 1955

C. E. AYRES
b. 1891   British scientist

A little inaccuracy saves a world of explanation.

Science, The False Messiah, 1927

BURT BACHARACH
1929–   American composer

A synonym is a word you use when you can't spell the word you first thought of.

quoted in Quote and Unquote, 1970

SIR FRANCIS BACON
1561–1626   British philosopher and statesman

Anger makes dull men witty – but it keeps them poor.

When should a man marry? A young man, not yet; an elder man, not at all. (cf. Diogenes)

'Of Marriage and Single Life'

'THE BAD AND THE BEAUTIFUL'

Elaine Stewart: There are no great men, buster. There are only men.
screenplay by Charles Schnee, 1952

JEAN BAECHLER
1937–   French writer

Every suicide is a solution to a problem.

Suicides, 1980

ARTHUR BAER
1897–1975   American writer

Alimony is like buying oats for a dead horse.

quoted in New York American

WALTER BAGEHOT
1826–1877 British economist and journalist

The cure for admiring the House of Lords is to go and look at it.

In my youth I hoped to do great things; now I shall be satisfied to get through without scandal.
> quoted in *Selected Letters of Raymond Chandler*,
> ed. F. MacShane, 1981

The most essential mental quality for a free people, whose liberty is to be progressive, permanent and on a large scale, is much stupidity.

One of the greatest pains to human nature is the pain of a new idea.

RUSSELL BAKER
1925– American humorist

The dirty work at political conventions is almost always done in the grim hours between midnight and dawn. Hangmen and politicians work best when the human spirit is at its lowest ebb.
> *The Sayings of Poor Russell*, 1972

Usually, terrible things that are done with the excuse that progress requires them are not really progress at all, but just terrible things.
> *Ibid.*

People who have the power to make things happen don't do the things that people do, so they don't know what needs to happen.
> *Ibid.*

A group of politicians deciding to dump a President because his morals are bad is like the Mafia getting together to bump off the Godfather for not going to church on Sunday.
> *New York Times*, 1974

Inanimate objects are classified scientifically into three major categories – those that don't work, those that break down and those that get lost.
> *New York Times*, 1968

People seem to enjoy things more when they know a lot of other people have been left out on the pleasure.
> *New York Times*, 1967

MICHAEL BAKUNIN
1814–1876   Russian anarchist

The smallest and most inoffensive state is still criminal in its dreams.

JAMES BALDWIN
1924–   American writer

The price one pays for pursuing any profession or calling is an intimate knowledge of its ugly side.

Nobody Knows My Name, 1961

Be careful what you set your heart upon – for it will surely be yours.

Ibid.

Children have never been very good at listening to their elders, but they have never failed to imitate them.

Esquire magazine, 1960

STANLEY BALDWIN
1867–1947   British Prime Minister

A platitude is simply a truth repeated till people get tired of hearing it.

quoted 1924

ARTHUR JAMES BALFOUR
1848–1930   British Prime Minister

It is unfortunate, considering enthusiasm moves the world, that so few enthusiasts can be trusted to speak the truth.

quoted 1918

attributed:

Nothing matters very much, and few things matter at all.

WHITNEY BALLIETT
1926–   American writer

A critic is a bundle of biases held loosely together by a sense of taste.

Dinosaurs in the Morning, 1962

HONORÉ DE BALZAC
1799–1850   French writer

The majority of husbands remind me of an orangutang trying to play the violin.

The Physiology of Marriage, 1828

Marriage must incessantly contend with a monster that devours everything: familiarity.

Ibid.

advice to sexually bored husbands:

Think of your mistress.

Ibid.

Believe everything you hear about the world; nothing is too impossibly bad.

Friendships last when each friend thinks he has a slight superiority over the other.

The duration of passion is proportionate with the original resistance of the woman.

Envy is the most stupid of vices, for there is no single advantage to be gained from it.

quoted in *Reflections on the Art of Life* by J. R. Solly, 1902

Manners are the hypocrisy of a nation.

TALLULAH BANKHEAD
1902–1968   American film star

It's the good girls who keep the diaries; the bad girls never have the time.

IMAMU AMIRI BARAKA (Leroi Jones)
1934–   American playwright

A rich man told me recently that a liberal is a man who tells other people what to do with their money.

quoted 1966

JULES-AMÉDÉE BARBEY D'AUREVILLY
1808–1889   French writer

In Paris, when God provides a beautiful woman, the devil at once retorts with a fool to keep her.

MAURICE BARING
1874–1945   British novelist and critic

There is no amount of praise which a man and an author cannot bear with equanimity. Some authors can even stand flattery.

Dead Letters, 1910

If you would know what the Lord God thinks of money, you have only to look at those to whom he gives it.

quoted in *Writers at Work*, 1st series, 1958

ALBEN W. BARKLEY
1877–1956   American senator

The best audience is intelligent, well-educated and a little drunk.

CLIVE BARNES
1927–   British drama critic

Television is the first truly democratic culture – the first culture available to everybody and entirely governed by what the people want. The most terrifying thing is what the people do want.

New York Times, 1969

MAURICE BARRÈS
1862–1923   French writer and politician

The politician is an acrobat: he keeps his balance by saying the opposite of what he does.

GERALD BARRY
b. 1899

Democracy: in which you say what you like and do what you're told.

JOHN BARRYMORE
1882–1942   American stage and screen actor

The good die young – because they see it's no use living if you've got to be good.

Sex: the thing that takes up the least amount of time and causes the most amount of trouble.

WAYNE R. BARTZ

The more ridiculous a belief system, the higher the probability of its success.

> quoted in *Human Behaviour* magazine, 1975

JACQUES BARZUN
1907–   American academic and writer

In any assembly the simplest way to stop the transacting of business and split the ranks is to appeal to a principle.

> *The House of Intellect*, 1959

BILL BATTIE
American sports coach

Class: when they're running you out of town, to look like you're leading the parade.

> *Sports Illustrated* magazine, 1976

CHARLES BAUDELAIRE
1821–1867   French poet

Life is a hospital in which every patient is possessed by the desire to change his bed.

Love is the desire to prostitute oneself. There is, indeed, no exalted pleasure that cannot be related to prostitution.

> *Intimate Journals*, 1887

What is irritating about love is that it is a crime that requires an accomplice.

VICKI BAUM
1888–1960   American writer

Marriage always demands the greatest understanding of the art of insincerity possible between two human beings.

And Life Goes On, 1931

PETER BEARD
1938–   American photographer

The whole world is a scab. The point is to pick it constructively.

quoted in *Loose Talk*, ed. L. Botts, 1980

You know what they say – the sweetest word in the English language is revenge.

Interview magazine, 1978

CECIL BEATON
1902–1980   British photographer

Perhaps the world's second worst crime is boredom. The first is being a bore.

PHILIPPE DE RÉMI, SIRE DE BEAUMANOIR
1246?–1296   French writer

Women, deceived by men, want to marry them; it is a kind of revenge as good as any other.

FRANCIS BEAUMONT and JOHN FLETCHER
1584–1616; 1579–1625   British playwrights

Oh love will make a dog howl in tune.

The Queen of Corinth

SIMONE DE BEAUVOIR
1908–   French writer

If you live long enough, you'll see that every victory turns into a defeat.

Tous les hommes sont mortels, 1946

What is an adult? A child blown up by age.

La Femme rompue, 1967

LORD BEAVERBROOK
1879–1964   Canadian-born British press magnate

Buy old masters. They fetch a better price than old mistresses.

SAMUEL BECKETT
1906–   Irish playwright and novelist

That desert of loneliness and recrimination that men call love.

quoted in *New York Review of Books*, 1971

The major sin is the sin of being born.

New York Herald Tribune, 1964

SIR THOMAS BEECHAM
1879–1961   British conductor

Criticism of the arts . . . taken by and large, ends in a display of suburban omniscience which sees no further than into the next-door garden.

Beecham Stories, 1978

A musicologist is a man who can read music but cannot hear it.

MAX BEERBOHM
1872–1956   British author and cartoonist

Most women are not as young as they are painted.

A Defence of Cosmetics

Anything that is worth doing has been done frequently. Things hitherto undone should be given, I suspect, a wide berth.

Mainly on the Air, 1946

BRENDAN BEHAN
1923–1964   Irish playwright

Critics are like eunuchs in a harem: they know how it's done, they've seen it done every day, but they're unable to do it themselves.

An author's first duty is to let down his country.

Guardian, 1960

SAUL BELLOW
1915–   American novelist

Take our politicians: they're a bunch of yo-yos. The presidency is now a cross between a popularity contest and a high school debate, with an encyclopedia of clichés as the first prize.

quoted 1980

ROBERT BENCHLEY
1889–1945   American humorist

A freelance is one who gets paid by the word – per piece or perhaps.

quoted in *Selected Letters of James Thurber*, ed. H. Thurber and J. Weeks, 1981

Drinking makes such fools of people, and people are such fools to begin with, that it's compounding a felony.

Everyone becomes the thing they most despise.

quoted in *Wit's End* by J. R. Gaines, 1977

ALAN BENNETT
1934–   British playwright

I have never understood this liking for war. It panders to instincts already catered for within the scope of any respectable domestic establishment.

Forty Years On

W. C. BENNETT
1905–1953   American clergyman

Blessed is he who expects no gratitude, for he shall not be disappointed.
quoted in *The Official Rules*, by P. Dickson, 1972

E. F. BENSON
1867–1940   British author

Even if a man was delightful, no woman would marry him if she knew what he was like.

Paul, 1906

JEREMY BENTHAM
1748–1832   British political theorist

When security and equality are in conflict, it will not do to hesitate a moment – equality must yield.

Principles of Legislation, 1789

Lawyers are the only persons in whom ignorance of the law is not punished.

ERIC BENTLEY
1916–   American writer

Ours is the age of substitutes: instead of language we have jargon; instead of principles, slogans; and, instead of genuine ideas, bright ideas.

The Dramatic Event, 1954

BERNARD BERENSON
1865–1959   American art historian

Consistency requires you to be as ignorant today as you were a year ago.

Notebook, 1892

We define genius as the capacity for productive reaction against one's training.

The Decline of Art

Governments last as long as the under-taxed can defend themselves against the over-taxed.

MILTON BERLE
1908– American comedian

A committee is a group that keeps the minutes and loses hours.

1954

SIR ISAIAH BERLIN
1909– British philosopher

When a man speaks of the need for realism one may be sure that this is always the prelude to some bloody deed.

quoted in *The Times*, 1981

HECTOR BERLIOZ
1803–1869 French composer

Time is a great teacher, but unfortunately it kills all its pupils.

Almanach des lettres françaises

LISA BERNBACH
American writer

Cynicism: an extension of ennui maintaining that not only are you bored, you are in a state of disbelief as well. And you cannot be convinced otherwise . . . more than a pose, it's also a handy time saver. By deflating your companion's enthusiasm, you can cut conversation in half.

The Official Preppy Handbook, 1981

ERIC BERNE
1910– American psychologist

We are born princes and the civilising process makes us frogs.

DANIEL BERRIGAN
1921– American radical

A revolution is interesting insofar as it avoids like the plague the plague it promised to heal.

New York Review of Books, 1971

ANEURIN BEVAN
1897–1960 British politician

I read the newspaper avidly. It is my one form of continuous fiction.

1960

In Germany democracy died by the headsman's axe. In Britain it can be by pernicious anaemia.

Righteous people terrify me . . . virtue is its own punishment.

GEORGES BIDAULT
1899– French politician

The weak have one weapon: the errors of those who think they are strong.

quoted in the *Observer*, 1962

AMBROSE BIERCE
1842–1913? American writer

Acquaintance, *n*: a person whom we know well enough to borrow from but not well enough to lend to. A degree of friendship called slight when the object is poor or obscure, and intimate when he is rich or famous.

The Devil's Dictionary, 1911

Alliance, *n*: in international politics, the union of two thieves who have their hands so deeply inserted into each other's pocket that they cannot safely plunder a third.

Ibid.

Ambition, *n*: an overmastering desire to be vilified by enemies while living and made ridiculous by friends when dead.

Ibid.

Applause, *n*: the echo of a platitude from the mouth of a fool.

Ibid.

Battle, *n*: a method of untying with the teeth a political knot that will not yield to the tongue.

Ibid.

Beauty, *n*: the power by which a woman charms a lover and terrifies a husband.

Ibid.

Bore, *n*: a person who talks when you wish him to listen.

Ibid.

Confidant, confidante, *n*: one entrusted by A with the secrets of B, confided to himself by C.

Ibid.

Conservative, *n*: a statesman who is enamoured of existing evils, as distinguished from the Liberal who wishes to replace them with others.

Ibid.

Cupid, *n*: the so-called god of love. This bastard creation of a barbarous fantasy . . . of all unbeautiful and inappropriate conceptions, this is the most reasonless and offensive.

Ibid.

Cynic, *n*: a blackguard whose faulty vision sees things as they are, not as they ought to be.

Ibid.

Destiny, *n*: a tyrant's excuse for crime and a fool's excuse for failure.

Ibid.

History, *n*: an account mostly false, of events mostly unimportant, which are brought about by rulers, mostly knaves, and soldiers mostly fools.

Ibid.

Insurrection, *n*: an unsuccessful revolution.

Ibid.

Labor, *n*: one of the processes whereby A acquires property for B.

Ibid.

Liberty, *n*: one of imagination's most precious possessions.

Ibid.

Love, *n*: a temporary insanity curable by marriage or the removal of the patient from the influences under which he incurred the disease . . . it is sometimes fatal, but more frequently to the physician than to the patient.

Ibid.

Male, *n*: a member of the unconsidered, or negligible sex. The male of the human race is commonly known to the female as Mere Man. The genus has two varieties: good providers and bad providers.

Ibid.

Marriage, *n*: the state or condition of a community consisting of a master, a mistress and two slaves, making in all, two.

Ibid.

Mythology, *n*: the body of a primitive people's beliefs, concerning its origin, early history, heroes, deities and so forth, as distinguished from the true accounts which it invents later.

Ibid.

Opposition, *n*: in politics the party that prevents the government from running amuck by hamstringing it.

Ibid.

Peace, *n*: in international affairs, a period of cheating between two periods of fighting.

Ibid.

Politics, *n*: a strife of interests masquerading as a contest of principles.

Ibid.

Rebel, *n*: the proponent of a new misrule who has failed to establish it.

Ibid.

Revolution, *n*: in politics, an abrupt change in the form of misgovernment.

Ibid.

Ugliness, *n*: a gift of the gods to certain women, entailing virtue without humility.

Ibid.

Wedding, *n*: a ceremony at which two persons undertake to become one, one undertakes to become nothing and nothing undertakes to become supportable.

Ibid.

JOSH BILLINGS (Henry Wheeler Shaw)
1818–1885   American humorist

Don't despise your poor relations, they may become suddenly rich one day.

DR L. BINDER
1927–

Confidence is simply that quiet, assured feeling you have before you fall flat on your face.

quoted in *Quote and Unquote*, 1970

ARTHUR BINSTEAD (The Pitcher)
1861–1914   British journalist

No modern woman with a grain of sense ever sends little notes to an unmarried man – not until she is married, anyway.

Pitcher's Proverbs, 1909

The great secret in life . . . [is] not to open your letters for a fortnight. At the expiration of that period you will find that nearly all of them have answered themselves.

Ibid.

Remorse is, after all, a thoroughly wholesome and healthy secretion. With what bitter anguish do we now recall those awful early virtues which we now know to have been only wasted opportunities.

Ibid.

It is a lamentable but incontrovertible solecism that many young men who are highly moral . . . are inwardly never happier than when suspected of disreputable tendencies.

Ibid.

The most serious doubt that has been thrown on the authenticity of the biblical miracles is the fact that most of the witnesses in regard to them were fishermen.

Ibid.

It must have been some unmarried fool that said 'A child can ask questions that a wise man cannot answer'; because, in any decent house, a brat that starts asking questions is promptly packed off to bed.

Ibid.

OTTO VON BISMARCK
1815–1898   German statesman

People never lie so much as after a hunt, during a war or before an election.

Universal suffrage is the government of a house by its nursery.

When you say you agree to a thing on principle, you mean that you have not the slightest intention of carrying it out in practice.

LADY BLESSINGTON
1789–1849   British hostess and author

Love matches are made by people who are content, for a month of honey, to condemn themselves to a life of vinegar.

JAMES BLISH
1921–1975   American writer

Credit . . . is the only enduring testimonial to man's confidence in man.

HERBERT BLOCK (Herblock)
1909–   American political cartoonist

If it's good, they'll stop making it.

NEIL BOGART
1943–   American rock music entrepreneur

If you hype something and it succeeds, you're a genius – it wasn't a hype. If you hype it and it fails, then it was just a hype.

NIELS BOHR
1885–1962 Danish physicist

An expert is a man who has made all the mistakes which can be made, in a very narrow field.

ROBERT BOLT
1924– British playwright

Morality's not practical. Morality's a gesture. A complicated gesture learnt from books.

A Man for All Seasons, 1962

CHRISTOPHER BOOKER
1937– British writer

The fashionable drawing rooms of London have always been happy to welcome outsiders – if only on their own, albeit undemanding terms. That is to say, artists, so long as they are not too talented, men of humble birth, so long as they have since amassed several million pounds, and socialists so long as they are Tories.

Now magazine, 1981

DANIEL J. BOORSTIN
1914– American writer

A best seller was a book which somehow sold well simply because it was selling well.

The Image, 1962

A sign of a celebrity is that his name is often worth more than his services.

Ibid.

. . . the messiness of experience, that may be what we mean by life.

Ibid.

JAMES H. BOREN
1925– American bureaucrat

When in doubt, mumble; when in trouble, delegate; when in charge, ponder.

quoted in *The Official Rules* by P. Dickson, 1972

JACQUES BOSSUET
1627–1704   French theologian

The cruellest revenge of a woman is to remain faithful to a man.

PAUL BOURGET
1852–1935   French writer

There is only one way to be happy by means of the heart – to have none.
La Physiologie de l'amour moderne, 1890

LORD BOYD-ORR
1880–1971   British politician

If people have to choose between freedom and sandwiches, they will take sandwiches.

F. H. BRADLEY
1846–1924   British writer

The propriety of some persons seems to consist in having improper thoughts about their neighbours.
Aphorisms, 1930

MARLON BRANDO
1924–   American film star

An actor's a guy who if you ain't talkin' about him, ain't listening.
Observer, 1956

J. BRÉCHEUX
French writer

The most delightful day after the one on which you buy a cottage in the country is the one on which you resell it.
quoted in *Reflections on the Art of Life* by J. R. Solly, 1902

BERTOLT BRECHT
1898–1956   German poet and playwright

Unhappy the land that needs heroes.

Galileo, 1943

Eats first, morals after.

The Threepenny Opera, 1928

What is robbing a bank compared with founding a bank?

Ibid.

How does a man live? By completely forgetting he is a human being.

Ibid.

Those who have had no share in the good fortunes of the mighty
Often have a share in their misfortunes.

The Caucasian Chalk Circle, 1945

War is like love, it always finds a way.

Mother Courage, 1939

You can only help one of your luckless brothers
By trampling down a dozen others.

The Good Person of Szechuan, 1943

When the leaders speak of peace
The common folk know
That war is coming
When the leaders curse war
The mobilization order is already written out.

Every day, to earn my daily bread
I go to the market where lies are bought
Hopefully
I take up my place among the sellers.

'Hollywood' in *Collected Poems 1913–1956*, 1976

On the wall in chalk is written
'They want war'
He who wrote it has already fallen.

Collected Poems 1913–1956, 1976

He who laughs has not yet heard the bad news.

GERALD BRENAN
1894– British essayist

Those who have some means think that the most important thing in the world is love. The poor know that it is money.

Thoughts in a Dry Season, 1978

JIMMY BRESLIN
1930– American writer

Football is a game designed to keep coalminers off the streets.

1973

AUSTEN BRIGGS
1931– American commercial artist

Let's remind ourselves that last year's fresh idea is today's cliché.

VERA BRITTAIN
1893–1970 British pacifist and writer

Politics are usually the executive expression of human immaturity.

The Rebel Passion, 1964

DAVID BRODER
1929– American journalist

Anybody that wants the presidency so much that he'll spend two years organising and campaigning for it is not to be trusted with the office.

Washington Post, 1973

COLM BROGAN
1902– British socialist

There is only one word for aid that is genuinely without strings and that word is blackmail.

SIR DENIS BROGAN
1900–1974   British historian

We all invent ourselves as we go along, and a great man's myths about himself tend to stick better than most.

KENNETH BROMFIELD
British advertising artist

From any cross-section of ads, the general advertiser's attitude would seem to be: if you are a lousy, smelly, idle, underprivileged and over-sexed status-seeking neurotic moron, give me your money.
Advertisers' Weekly, 1962

LOUISE BROOKS
1900–   American film star

Most beautiful but dumb girls think they are smart and get away with it, because other people, on the whole, aren't much smarter.
quoted in *Show People* by K. Tynan, 1980

MEL BROOKS
1927–   American comedian and film director

Usually, when a lot of men get together, it's called war.
The Listener, 1978

If Presidents don't do it to their wives, they do it to the country.
as the Two-Thousand-Year-Old Man

LORD BROUGHAM
1778–1868   British politician

A lawyer is a learned gentleman who rescues your estate from your enemies and keeps it for himself.

HEYWOOD BROUN
1888–1939   American journalist

The most prolific period of pessimism comes at twenty-one, or thereabouts, when the first attempt is made to translate dreams into reality.

Pieces of Hate, 1922

History is largely concerned with arranging good entrances for people and later exits not always quite so good.

Ibid.

Free speech is about as good a cause as the world has ever known. But it . . . gets shoved aside in favour of things which seem at a given moment more vital . . . everybody favours free speech in the slack moments when no axes are being ground.

1926

Just as every conviction begins as a whim so does every emancipator serve his apprenticeship as a crank. A fanatic is a great leader who is just entering the room.

1928

The urge to gamble is so universal and its practice so pleasurable that I assume it must be evil.

THOMAS BROWN
1830–1897   Manx poet

A rich man's joke is always funny.

LENNY BRUCE
1923–1966   American comedian

Now a Jew, in the dictionary, is one who is descended from the ancient tribes of Judea . . . but you and I know what a Jew is – one who killed Our Lord . . . A lot of people say to me 'Why did you kill Christ?' 'I dunno, it was one of those parties, got out of hand, you know . . .' We killed him because he didn't want to become a doctor, that's why we killed him.

quoted in *The Essential Lenny Bruce*, ed. J. Cohen, 1967

Satire is tragedy plus time.

Ibid.

I know what 'custody' [of the children] means. 'Get even'. That's all custody means. Get even with your old lady.

Ibid.

I'll be comfortable on the couch. Famous last words.

Ibid.

Never tell. Not if you love your wife . . . In fact, if your old lady walks in on you, deny it. Yeah. Just flat out and she'll believe it: 'I'm tellin' ya. This chick came downstairs with a sign around her neck "Lay On Top Of Me Or I'll Die". I didn't know what I was gonna do . . .'

Ibid.

If you're going to break up with your old lady and you live in a small town, make sure you don't break up at three in the morning. Because you're screwed – there's nothing to do . . . So make it about nine in the morning, . . . bullshit around, worry her a little, then come back at seven in the night.

Ibid.

The liberals can understand everything but people who don't understand them.

The whole motivation for any performer: 'Look at me, Ma!'

In the Halls of Justice the only justice is in the halls.

GEORGE BUCHANAN
1904–   British novelist

Without the skeleton at the feast, it is questionable whether the feast tastes good.

WILLIAM F. BUCKLEY, Jr.
1925–   American editor and diplomat

Idealism is fine, but as it approaches reality the cost becomes prohibitive.

CHARLES BUKOWSKI
1920–   American poet and author

Love is a way with some meaning; sex is meaning enough.

Notes of a Dirty Old Man, 1969

Of course it's possible to love a human being if you don't know them too well.

Ibid.

What's the difference between a guy in the bighouse and the average guy you pass in the street? The guy in the bighouse is a Loser who tried.

Ibid.

The difference between a Democracy and a Dictatorship is that in a Democracy you vote first and take orders later; in a Dictatorship you don't have to waste your time voting.

Erections, Ejaculations, Exhibitions and Tales of Ordinary Madness, 1972

LUTHER BURBANK
1849–1926   American naturalist

For those who do not think, it is best to rearrange their prejudices once in a while.

ANTHONY BURGESS
1917–   British author

The possession of a book becomes a substitute for reading it.

New York Times Book Review, 1966

EDMUND BURKE
1729–1797   British statesman and author

All oppressors attribute the frustration of their desires to the want of sufficient rigour. Then they redouble the efforts of their impotent cruelty.

The Impeachment of Warren Hastings, 1788

It is a general error to suppose the loudest complainer for the public to be the most anxious for its welfare.

By a revolution in the state, the fawning sycophant of yesterday is converted into the austere critic of the present hour.

Reflections on the Revolution in France, 1790

If any ask me what a free government is, I answer that for any practical purposes, it is what the people think so.

LEO J. BURKE

The husband who doesn't tell his wife everything probably reasons that what she doesn't know won't hurt him.

> quoted in *Peter's Quotations*, ed. Dr L. Peter, 1977

CHESTER BURNETT (Howlin' Wolf)
1910–1976   American musician

One time you let people know how much sense you got, right away they quit having anything to do with you.

GEORGE BURNS
1896–   American comedian

Too bad all the people who know how to run the country are busy driving cabs and cutting hair.

WILLIAM S. BURROUGHS
1914–   American writer

1. Never give anything away for nothing. 2. Never give more than you have to (always catch the buyer hungry and always make him wait). 3. Always take back everything if you possibly can.

> on drug pushing, *Daily Telegraph*, 1964

A paranoid is a man who knows a little of what's going on.

> *Friends* magazine, 1970

The police and so forth only exist insofar as they can demonstrate their authority. They say they're here to preserve order, but in fact they'd go absolutely mad if all the criminals of the world went on strike for a month. They'd be on their knees begging for a crime. That's the only existence they have.

> *Guardian*, 1969

WILHELM BUSCH
1832–1908   German cartoonist

The good (I am convinced, for one)
Is but the bad one leaves undone.

Bilderbogen

Once your reputation's done
You can live a life of fun.

'Pious Helene'

DR DAVID BUTLER
1924–   British psephologist

The function of the expert is not to be more right than other people,
but to be wrong for more sophisticated reasons.

Observer, 1969

SAMUEL BUTLER
1612–1680   British satirist and poet

The reasons why fools and knaves thrive better in the world than wiser
and honester men is because they are nearer to the general temper of
mankind, which is nothing but a mixture of cheat and folly.

Prose Observations, 1660–80

There are more fools than knaves in the world, else the knaves would
not have enough to live on.

SAMUEL BUTLER
1835–1902   British author

'Home Sweet Home' must surely have been written by a bachelor.

The course of true anything never does run smooth.

Notebooks, 1912

Some men love truth so much that they seem to be in continual fear
lest she should catch a cold on overexposure.

Ibid.

Marriage is distinctly and repeatedly excluded from heaven. Is this
because it is thought likely to mar the general felicity?

Ibid.

Any fool can tell the truth, but it requires a man of some sense to
know how to lie well.

God cannot alter the past, that is why he is obliged to connive at the
existence of historians.

37

If God considered woman a fit helpmeet for man, he must have had a very poor opinion of man.

The tendency of modern science is to reduce proof to absurdity by continually reducing absurdity to proof.

All progress is based upon a universal innate desire of every organism to live beyond its income.

Notebooks, 1912

MICHEL BUTOR
1926–   French writer

Our daily life is a bad serial by which we let ourselves be bewitched.

Répertoire II

GEORGE GORDON, LORD BYRON
1788–1824   British poet

Now hatred is by far the longest pleasure;
Men love in haste, but they detest at leisure.

Don Juan, 1819–24

In her first passion woman loves her lover,
In all the others all she loves is love.

Ibid.

One of the pleasures of reading old letters is the knowledge that they need no answer.

quoted in *The Oxford Book of Aphorisms*, ed. J. Gross, 1983

JAMES BRANCH CABELL
1878–1959   American writer

The optimist proclaims we live in the best of all possible worlds; and the pessimist fears this is true.

The Silver Stallion, 1926

GAIUS JULIUS CAESAR
100–44 BC   Roman general and statesman

All bad precedents began as justifiable measures.

quoted in *The Conspiracy of Catiline* by Sallust, 1st century BC

SID CAESAR
1922–   American comedian

The trouble with telling a good story is that it invariably reminds the other fellow of a dull one.

SIMON CAMERON
1799–1889   American politician

An honest politician is one who when he is bought will stay bought.

ROY CAMPBELL
1902–1957   British poet

Translations (like wives) are seldom faithful if they are in the least attractive.

Poetry Review, 1949

ALBERT CAMUS
1913–1960   French writer

Every revolutionary ends up by becoming either an oppressor or a heretic.

The Rebel, 1951

The slave begins by demanding justice and ends by wanting to wear a crown. He must dominate in his turn.

Ibid.

The future is the only kind of property that the masters willingly concede to slaves.

Ibid.

He who despairs over an event is a coward, but he who holds hopes for the human condition is a fool.

Notebooks, 1962

Politics and the fate of mankind are shaped by men without ideals and without greatness. Men who have greatness within them don't go in for politics.

Ibid.

The revolution as myth is the definitive revolution.

Ibid.

Those who write clearly have readers; those who write obscurely have commentators.

ELIAS CANETTI
1905–   Bulgarian writer

Success listens only to applause. To all else it is deaf.

The name 'moralist' sounds like a perversion, one wouldn't be surprised at finding it suddenly in Krafft-Ebing.

The Human Province, 1978

GEORGE CANNING
1770–1827   British Prime Minister

Give me the avowed, the erect, the manly foe,
Bold I can meet – perhaps may turn his blow!

But of all plagues, good Heaven, thy wrath can send,
Save me, oh save me from the candid friend.

JIMMY CANNON
1890–1974   American sports writer

Fishing, with me, has always been an excuse to drink in the daytime.
quoted in No Cheering in the Pressbox *by J. Holtzman, 1973*

ALFRED CAPUS
1858–1922   French writer

To marry a woman who you love and who loves you is to pay a wager
with her as to who will stop loving the other first.
Notes et pensées, 1926

THOMAS CARLYLE
1795–1881   British historian and essayist

Happy are the people whose annals are blank in the history books.
Frederick the Great, 1858–65

The public is an old woman. Let her maunder and mumble.

JACK CARSON
1910–1963   American actor

A fan club is a group of people who tell an actor he is not alone in
the way he feels about himself.
quoted in The Wit of the Theatre, *ed. R. May, 1969*

ROBERT CARSON
1918–

Television . . . the longest amateur night in history.
quoted in The Filmgoer's Book of Quotes, *ed. L. Halliwell, 1973*

WYNN CATLIN
1930–   American writer

Democracy is the art of saying 'Nice doggie' until you can find a rock.

DICK CAVETT
1936– American television personality

As long as people will accept crap, it will be financially profitable to dispense it.

Playboy magazine, 1971

LOUIS-FERDINAND CÉLINE
1894–1961 French writer

If you aren't rich you should always look useful.

Journey to the End of the Night, 1932

SIR PAUL CHAMBERS
1904–1981 British industrialist

Exhortation of other people to do something is the last resort of politicians who are at a loss to know what to do themselves.

1961

NICOLAS CHAMFORT
1741–1794 French writer

The only thing that stops God sending a second Flood is that the first one was useless.

Characters and Anecdotes, 1771

Change in fashion is the tax which the industry of the poor levies on the vanity of the rich.

Bachelors' wives and old maids' children are always perfect.

The success of many books is due to the affinity betwen the mediocrity of the author's ideas and those of the public.

quoted in *A Cynic's Breviary* by J. R. Solly, 1925

Conscience is a cur that does not stop us from passing but that we cannot prevent from barking.

Ibid.

Love, in present day society, is just the exchange of two momentary desires and the contact of two skins.

Maximes et pensées, 1805

'CHAMPION'

Paul Stewart: [Boxing] . . . is the only sport in the world where two guys get paid for doing something they'd be arrested for if they got drunk and did it for nothing.

screenplay by Carl Foreman, 1949

RAYMOND CHANDLER
1888–1959 American writer

Organised crime is just the dirty side of the sharp dollar.

The Long Good-bye, 1953

Cops never say good-bye. They're always hoping to see you again in the line-up.

Ibid.

[The] constant yelping about a free press means, with a few honourable exceptions, freedom to peddle scandal, crime, sex, sensationalism, hate, innuendo and the political financial uses of propaganda. A newspaper is a business out to make money through advertising revenue. That is predicated on its circulation and you know what circulation depends on.

Ibid.

The law isn't justice. It's a very imperfect mechanism. If you press exactly the right buttons and are also lucky, justice may also turn up in the answer.

Ibid.

Alcohol is like love: the first kiss is magic, the second is intimate, the third is routine. After that you just take the girl's clothes off.

Ibid.

MAURICE CHAPELAIN
1906– French writer

The final delusion is the belief that one has lost all delusions.

Main courante

GEORGE CHAPMAN
1559–1634   British poet and playwright

Young men think old men are fools; but old men know young men
are fools.

All Fools, 1605

JOHN JAY CHAPMAN
1862–1933   American diplomat

Organised hatred, that is unity.

'Lines on the Death of Bismarck', 1898

ALEXANDER CHASE
1926–   American journalist

People, like sheep, tend to follow a leader – occasionally in the right
direction.

Perspectives, 1966

For the unhappy man death is the commutation of a sentence of life
imprisonment.

Ibid.

GEOFFREY CHAUCER
1343?–1400   British poet

Filth and old age, I'm sure you will agree,
Are powerful wardens upon chastity.

The Canterbury Tales, 1387–1400

MALCOLM DE CHAZAL
1902–   French writer

The family is a court of justice which never shuts down for night or
day.

Sens plastique, 1949

ANTON CHEKHOV
1860–1904   Russian playwright

If you are afraid of loneliness, don't marry.

VICTOR CHERBULIEZ
1829–1899   French writer

To repent, and then to start all over again, such is life.

> quoted in *A Cynic's Breviary* by J. R. Solly, 1925

LORD CHESTERFIELD
1694–1773   British politician and correspondent

Be wiser than other people if you can, but do not tell them so.

> letter to his son, 1745

As fathers commonly go, it is seldom a misfortune to be fatherless; and considering the general run of sons, as seldom a misfortune to be childless.

The only solid and lasting peace between a man and his wife is, doubtless, a separation.

> letter to his son, 1763

Distrust all those who love you extremely upon a very slight acquaintance and without any visible reason.

Modesty is the only sure bait when you angle for praise.

If the multitude ever deviate into the right, it is always for the wrong reasons.

G. K. CHESTERTON
1874–1936   British novelist and critic

The artistic temperament is a disease that afflicts amateurs.

> *Heretics*, 1905

Democracy means government by the uneducated, while aristocracy means government by the badly educated.

> *New York Times*, 1931

Thieves respect property; they merely wish the property to become their property that they may more perfectly respect it.

> *The Man Who Was Thursday*, 1908

'My country, right or wrong' is a thing that no patriot would think of saying, except in a desperate case. It is like saying 'My mother, drunk or sober.'

> *The Defendant*

English experience indicates that when two great political parties agree about something, it is generally wrong.

1919

The full potentialities of human fury cannot be reached until a friend of both parties tactfully interferes.

MAURICE CHEVALIER
1888–1972 French singer and film star

Many a man has fallen in love with a girl in a light so dim he would not have chosen a suit by it.

195

CHARLES CHINCHOLLES
1845–1902 French aphorist

That all men should be brothers is the dream of people who have no brothers.

Pensées de tout le monde, 188

The great merit of society is to make one appreciate solitude.

quoted in *Reflections on the Art of Life* by J. R. Solly, 190

DR BROCK CHISHOLM
d. 1948 American physician

Conscience is what your mother told you before you were six years old.

quoted in *Ladies' Home Journal*, 194

CHOU EN LAI
1898–1976 Chinese politician

All diplomacy is a continuation of war by other means.

19

ROBERT CHRISTGAU
1945– American rock music critic

The old complaint that mass culture is designed for eleven-year-olds of course a shameful canard. The key age has traditionally been more like fourteen.

Esquire magazine, 1969

SIR WINSTON CHURCHILL
1874–1965 British statesman

Broadly speaking, human beings may be divided into three classes: those who are billed to death, those who are worried to death and those who are bored to death.

A prisoner of war is a man who tries to kill you and fails, and then asks you not to kill him.

1952

We must beware of needless innovations, especially when guided by logic.

1942

Too often the strong, silent man is silent only because he does not know what to say, and is reputed strong only because he has remained silent.

1924

Political skill . . . the ability to foretell what is going to happen tomorrow, next week, next month and next year. And to have the ability afterwards to explain why it didn't happen.

quoted in 1965

An appeaser is one who feeds a crocodile – hoping that it will eat him last.

1954

JOHN CIARDI
1916– American poet

Gentility is what is left over from rich ancestors after the money is gone.

Saturday Review

MARCUS TULLIUS CICERO
106–43 BC   Roman lawyer and philosopher

There is no fortress so strong that money cannot take it.

There is no opinion so absurd that some philosopher will not express it.

Persistence in one opinion has never been considered a merit in political leaders.

Ad familiares, 1st century BC

E. M. CIORAN
1911–   French philosopher

To be modern is to potter about in the terminal ward.

Syllogismes de l'amertume, 1952

The history of ideas is the history of the grudges of solitary men.

Ibid.

All that shimmers on the surface of the world, all that we call interesting, is the fruit of ignorance and inebriation.

The Fall into Time, 1971

No-one recovers from the disease of being born, a deadly wound if ever there was one.

Ibid.

The hour of their crime does not strike simultaneously for all nations. This explains the permanence of history.

quoted in *The Faber Book of Aphorisms*,
ed. Auden and Kronenberger, 1964

Tyrants are always assassinated too late. That is their great excuse.

Since all life is futility, then the decision to exist must be the most irrational of all.

The Temptation to Exist, 1956

KENNETH CLARK, Lord Clark
1903–1983   British art historian

It is chiefly through the instinct to kill that man achieves intimacy with the life of nature.

ARTHUR C. CLARKE
1917–   American science writer

When a distinguished but elderly scientist states that something is possible, he is almost certainly right. When he states that something is impossible, he is very probably wrong.

Profile of the Future, 1973

PAUL CLAUDEL
1868–1955   French playwright and poet

People are only heroes when they can't do anything else.

Journal

GEORGES CLEMENCEAU
1841–1929   French statesman

War is a series of catastrophes which result in a victory.

ALEXANDER COCKBURN
1945–   British journalist

The First Law of Journalism: to confirm existing prejudice, rather than contradict it.

(more) magazine, 1974

SIR BARNETT COCKS
1907–   British scientist

A committee is a cul-de-sac down which ideas are lured and then quietly strangled.

New Scientist, 1973

JEAN COCTEAU
1889–1963   French man of letters

Tact consists in knowing how far to go in going too far.

quoted in *The Faber Book of Aphorisms*,
ed. Auden and Kronenberger, 1964

The greatest masterpiece in literature is only a dictionary out of order.

Le Potomak

We must believe in luck. For how else can we explain the success of those we don't like?

What is history after all? History is facts which become legend in the end; legends are lies which become history in the end.

1957

NIK COHN
1946– British writer

Generation to generation . . . nothing changes in Bohemia.

Awopbopaloobopalopbamboom, 1969

GEORGE COLEMAN THE ELDER
1732–1794 British playwright

Love and a cottage, eh, Fanny! Ah, give me indifference and a coach and six!

The Clandestine Marriage, 1766

SAMUEL TAYLOR COLERIDGE
1772–1834 British poet

Swans sings before they die – 'twere no bad thing
Did certain persons die before they sing.

'Epigram on a Volunteer Singer'

COLETTE (Sidonie-Gabrielle Colette)
1873–1954 French novelist

The only really masterful noise a man makes in a house is the noise of his key, when he is still on the landing, fumbling for the lock.

quoted in *The Wit of Women*

JOHN CHURTON COLLINS
1848–1908 British critic

In prosperity our friends know us; in adversity we know our friends.

CHARLES CALEB COLTON
1780–1832 British writer and clergyman

Genius, in one respect, is like gold; numbers of persons are constantly writing about both, who have neither.

When the million applaud, you ask yourself what harm you have done; when they censure you, what good.

Lawyers are the only civil delinquents whose judges must of necessity be chosen from themselves.

IVY COMPTON-BURNETT
1884–1969 British novelist

There is probably nothing like living together for blinding people to each other.

Mother and Son, 1955

RICHARD CONDON
1915– American novelist

It is the rule, not the exception, that otherwise unemployable public figures inevitably take to writing for publication.

WILLIAM CONGREVE
1670–1729 British playwright

'Tis an unhappy circumstance that . . . the man so often should outlive the lover.

The Way of the World, 1700

Courtship to marriage, as a very witty prologue to a very dull play.

The Old Bachelor, 1693

SENATOR ROSCOE CONKLING
1829–1888 American politician

When Dr. Johnson defined patriotism as the last refuge of a scoundrel, he ignored the enormous possibilities of the word reform.

1876

JOHN CONNALLY
1917–   American politician

When you're out of office, then you can be a statesman.

1971

CYRIL CONNOLLY (Palinurus)
1903–1975   British writer and critic

Destroy him as you will, the bourgeois always bounces up. Execute him, expropriate him, starve him out *en masse*, and he reappears in your children.

1937

Those whom the gods wish to destroy, they first call promising.
Enemies of Promise, 1938

All charming people have something to conceal, usually their total dependence on the appreciation of others.

Ibid.

There is no more sombre enemy of good art than the pram in the hall.

Ibid.

The civilised are those who get more out of life than the uncivilised, and for this the uncivilised have not forgiven them.
The Unquiet Grave, 1945

There is no fury like an ex-wife searching for a new lover.

Ibid.

We must select the illusion which appeals to our temperament and embrace it with passion, if we want to be happy.

Ibid.

The dread of loneliness is greater than the fear of bondage, so we get married.

Ibid.

The civilisation of one epoch becomes the manure of the next.

Ibid.

Life is a maze in which we take the wrong turning before we have learnt to walk.

Ibid.

Our memories are card indexes consulted, and then put back in disorder by authorities whom we do not control.

quoted in The Faber Book of Aphorisms,
ed. Auden and Kronenberger, 1964

The bestseller is the golden touch of mediocre talent.

Journal and Memoir, ed. D. Pryce-Jones, 1983

Always be nice to those younger than you, because they are the ones who will be writing about you.

Ibid.

The greatest problem with women is how to contrive that they should seem our equals.

Ibid.

The romantic is a spoilt priest, just as the novelist is a spoilt poet.

Ibid.

Youth is a period of missed opportunities.

Ibid

The artist is a member of the leisured classes who cannot pay for his leisure.

Ibid.

Only two things are worth having – money which you have not had the trouble of earning, and irresponsibility.

Ibid.

The past is the only dead thing that smells sweet.

Ibid.

English Law: where there are two alternatives: one intelligent, one stupid; one attractive, one vulgar; one noble, one ape-like; one serious and sincere, one undignified and false; one far-sighted, one short; EVERYBODY will INVARIABLY choose the latter.

Ibid.

The only way for writers to meet is to share a quick pee over a common lamp-post.

Ibid.

A lot of pain and nuisance might be avoided if the rich would only appreciate the point where love becomes money.

Ibid.

JOSEPH CONRAD (Jozef Korzeniowski)
1857–1924   Anglo-Polish novelist

The revolutionary spirit is mightily convenient in this: that it frees one from all scruples as regards ideas.

JILLY COOPER
1937–   British journalist and novelist

Like Mariana of the moated Grange, who hated late afternoon most of all, the unfaithful wife dreads the coming of 5.30, when the danger zone of her husband returning home has been entered and she knows now it's too late for the lover to telephone.

The British in Love, 1980

The working classes have a reputation for potency and being good in bed – a myth probably started by middle-class novelists and by graphologists who claim that anyone with loopy writing must be highly sexed.

Class, 1979

ALAN COREN
1938–   British humorist

Democracy consists of choosing your dictators, after they've told you what it is you think you want to hear.

Daily Mail, 1975

Television is more interesting than people. If it were not, we should have people standing in the corners of our rooms.

quoted in *The Penguin Dictionary of Modern Quotations*,
ed. J. and M. Cohen, 1981

F. M. CORNFORD
1874–1943   British writer

Propaganda is that branch of the art of lying which consists in nearly deceiving your friends without quite deceiving your enemies.
(cf. Walter Lippmann)

New Statesman, 1978

HART CRANE
1899–1932   American poet

Love . . . a burnt match skating in a urinal.

'The Bridge'

MANDELL CREIGHTON
1843–1901   British clergyman

No people do so much harm as those who go about doing good.

QUENTIN CRISP
1908–   British autobiographer

Decency . . . must be an even more exhausting state to maintain than its opposite. Those who succeed seem to need a stupefying amount of sleep.

The Naked Civil Servant, 1968

The young always have the same problem – how to rebel and conform at the same time. They have now solved this by defying their parents and copying one another.

Ibid.

Though the strongest resist all temptation, all human beings who suffer from any deficiency, real or imagined, are under compulsion to draw attention to it.

Ibid.

There are three reasons for becoming a writer: the first is that you need the money; the second that you have something to say that you think the world should know; the third is that you can't think what to do with the long winter evenings.

Ibid.

To know all is not to forgive all. It is to despise everybody.

Ibid.

The *vie de bohème* is a way of life that has two formidable enemies – time and marriage. Even hooligans marry, though they know that marriage is but for a little while. It is alimony that is for ever.

Ibid.

The English think that incompetence is the same thing as sincerity.

New York Times, 1977

Never keep up with the Joneses. Drag them down to your level, it's cheaper.

1978

It is explained that all relationships require a little give and take. This is untrue. Any partnership demands that we give and give and give and at the last, as we flop into our graves exhausted, we are told that we didn't give enough.

How to Become a Virgin, 1981

If any reader of this book is in the grip of some habit of which he is deeply ashamed, I advise him not to give way to it in secret but to do it on television. No-one will pass him with averted gaze on the other side of the street. People will cross the road at the risk of losing their own lives in order to say 'We saw you on the telly.'

Ibid.

Nothing shortens a journey so pleasantly as an account of misfortunes at which the hearer is permitted to laugh.

Ibid.

The very purpose of existence is to reconcile the glowing opinion we hold of ourselves with the appalling things that other people think about us.

Ibid.

OLIVER CROMWELL
1599–1658   Lord Protector of England

remarking on the crowds cheering his progress:

The people would be just as noisy if they were going to see me hanged.

Necessity hath no law.

1654

ELY CULBERTSON
1891–1956   American bridge champion

Power politics is the diplomatic name for the law of the jungle.

Must We Fight Russia?, 1946

E. E. CUMMINGS
1894–1962   American poet

Take the socalled 'standardofliving'. What do most people mean by
'living'? They don't mean living. They mean the latest and closest
plural approximation to the singular prenatal passivity which science,
in its finite but unbounded wisdom, has succeeded in selling their
wives.

Poems, 1954

SAM CUMMINGS
American arms dealer

The arms business is founded on human folly, that is why its depths
will never be plumbed and why it will go on forever. All weapons
are defensive and all spare parts are non-lethal. The plainest print
cannot be read through a solid gold sovereign, or a ruble or a golden
eagle.

1978

CHARLES P. CURTIS
1891–1959   American lawyer

Fraud is the homage that force pays to reason.

A Commonplace Book, 1957

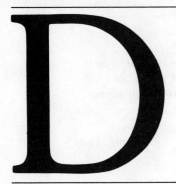

RICHARD M. DALEY
1902–1975   American mayor

advising on the safe enjoyment of graft:

Don't take a nickel, just hand them your business card.

CHARLES DARLING
1849–1936   British lawyer

If a man stay away from his wife for seven years, the law presumes the separation to have killed him; yet according to our daily experience, it might well prolong his life.

Scintillae Juris, 1877

CYRIL DEAN DARLINGTON
1903–   British biologist

Mankind . . . will not willingly admit that its destiny can be revealed by the breeding of flies or the counting of chiasmata.

lecture, 1960

CLARENCE DARROW
1857–1938   American lawyer and reformer

I am a friend of the working man, and I would rather be his friend than be one.

The first half of our lives is ruined by our parents, and the second half by our children.

When I was a boy I was told that anyone could become President. I'm beginning to believe it.

BETTE DAVIS
1908–   American film star

remarking on a passing starlet:

There goes the good time that was had by all.

DR EDWARD DE BONO
1933–   British writer

Unhappiness is best defined as the difference between our talents and our expectations.

Observer, 1977

CHARLES DE GAULLE
1890–1970   French statesman and general

Treaties are like roses and young girls – they last while they last.

1963

In order to become the master, the politician poses as the servant.

1969

Since a politician never believes what he says, he is surprised when others believe him.

1962

GUY DELAFOREST
1833–?   French aphorist

Life is a lease imposed upon the occupant without previous communication of the conditions in the contract.

quoted in *Reflections on the Art of Life* by J. R. Solly, 1902

Between time and ourselves, it is a struggle as to which shall kill the other.

Ibid.

CASIMIR DELAVIGNE
1793–1843   French poet and playwright

Ever since Adam fools have been in the majority.

HUGO DEMARTINI
1931– Czech artist

People are always talking about tradition, but they forget we have a tradition of a few hundred years of nonsense and stupidity, that there is a tradition of idiocy, incompetence and crudity.

1968, quoted in Contemporary Artists, 1977

NIGEL DENNIS
1912– British writer

It is usually a mistake to confuse the author's point of view with the form he has discovered for it. When the second is admirable, we give him the Nobel Prize for the first.

quoted in New York Review of Books, 1971

LORD DERBY
1799–1869 British Prime Minister

. . . the duty of an opposition [is] very simple – to oppose everything and propose nothing.

1841

VITTORIO DE SICA
1901–1974 Italian film director

Moral indignation is in most cases 2 percent moral, 48 percent indignation and 50 percent envy.

Observer, 1961

VIRGINIE DES RIEUX
French writer

Marriage is a lottery in which men stake their liberty and women their happiness.

PETER DE VRIES
1910– American writer

If there's one major cause for the spread of mass illiteracy, it's the fact that everybody can read and write.

The Tents of Wickedness, 1959

LORD THOMAS DEWAR
1864–1930   Scottish distiller

Confessions may be good for the soul, but they are bad for the reputation.

Four fifths of the perjury in the world is expended on tombstones, women and competitors.

No woman can endure a gambling husband, unless he is a steady winner.

CHARLES D'HÉRICAULT
1823–1899   French aphorist

Lord, defend me from my friends; I can account for my enemies.
quoted in *A Cynic's Breviary* by J. R. Solly, 1925

PAUL DICKSON
1939–   American writer

Rowe's Rule: the odds are five to six that the light at the end of the tunnel is the headlight of an oncoming train.
The Official Rules, 1978

Carson's Consolation: no experiment is ever a complete failure. It can always be used as a bad example.
Ibid.

DENIS DIDEROT
1713–1784   French philosopher and encyclopaedist

Every day men sleep with women they do not love and do not sleep with women whom they do love.
Jacques le fataliste, 1773

JOAN DIDION
1934–   American writer

There is always one thing to remember: writers are always selling somebody out.
Slouching Towards Bethlehem, 1968

Innocence ends when one is stripped of the delusion that one likes oneself.

On Self Respect, 1961

PHYLLIS DILLER
1917–   American comedienne

Cleaning your house while your kids are still growing is like shovelling the walk before it stops snowing.

DIOGENES
c. 400 – *c*. 325 BC   Greek philosopher

asked when a man should marry:

For a young man, not yet: for an old man, never at all.
(cf. Sir Francis Bacon)

BENJAMIN DISRAELI
1804–1881   British Prime Minister and novelist

The conduct and opinions of public men at different periods of their careers must not be curiously contrasted in a free and aspiring society.

speech, 1834

What we call public opinion is generally public sentiment.

speech, 1880

The disappointment of manhood succeeds to the delusion of youth.

No man is regular in his attendance at the House of Commons until he is married.

He who anticipates his century is generally persecuted when living and is always pilfered when dead.

Something unpleasant is coming when men are anxious to tell the truth.

If every man were straightforward in his opinions, there would be no conversation.

There is no act of treachery or mean-ness of which a political party is not capable; for in politics there is no honour.

Vivian Grey, 1824

on dealing with the Royal Family:

I never deny, I never contradict. I sometimes forget.

The magic of our first love is our ignorance that it can ever end.

Every woman should marry – and no man.

Lothair, 1870

A majority is always the best repartee.

Tancred, 1847

It is well known what a middle man is: he is a man who bamboozles one party and plunders the other.

speech, 1845

Youth is a blunder, manhood a struggle, old age a regret.

Coningsby, 1844

J. FRANK DOBIE
1888–1964 American writer

The average Ph.D thesis is nothing but the transference of bones from one graveyard to another.

A Texan in England, 1945

L. DOCQUIER
French aphorist

The animals are not as stupid as one thinks – they have neither doctors nor lawyers.

quoted in *Reflections on the Art of Life* by J. R. Solly, 1902

J. P. DONLEAVY
1926– American writer

Writing is turning one's worst moments into money.

quoted 1968

LORD ALFRED DOUGLAS
1870–1945   British poet

It pays in England to be a revolutionary and a bible-smacker most of one's life, and then come round.

1938

NORMAN DOUGLAS
1886–1952   British writer

Education is a state-controlled manufactory of echoes.

How about Europe

To find a friend one must close one eye; to keep him – two.

An Almanac

DR RUDOLF DREIKURS
1897–   German psychologist

The complaints which anyone voices against his mate indicate exactly the qualities which stimulated attraction before marriage.

The Challenge of Marriage, 1946

GUSTAVE DROZ
1832–1895   French aphorist

One is often kept in the right road by a rut.

quoted in *Reflections on the Art of Life* by J. R. Solly, 1902

PETER DRUCKER
1909–   American management theorist

So much of what we call management consists in making it difficult for people to work.

HUGH DRUMMOND
British aristocrat

Ladies and Gentlemen, I give you a toast. It is: Absinthe makes the tart grow fonder!

quoted in *The Vintage Years* by S. Hicks, 1943

JOHN DRYDEN
1631–1700   British poet

Here lies my wife: here let her lie!
Now she's at rest, and so am I.

epitaph intended for his wife

All heiresses are beautiful.

No government has ever been, or can ever be, wherein time-servers
and blockheads will not be uppermost.

ALEXANDRE DUMAS *père*
1803–1870   French writer

We blame in others only those faults by which we do not profit.

ALEXANDRE DUMAS *fils*
1824–1895   French writer

I prefer rogues to imbeciles, because they sometimes take a rest.

If God were suddenly condemned to live the life which he has inflicted
upon men, he would kill himself.

Pensées d'album

NELL DUNN
1936–   British writer

When you're married to someone, they take you for granted . . . when
you're living with someone it's fantastic . . . they're so frightend of losing
you they've got to keep you satisfied all the time.

Poor Cow

FINLAY PETER DUNNE
1867–1936   American humorist

The American nation in the sixth ward is a fine people; they love the
eagle – on the back of a dollar.

Trust everybody, but cut the cards.

Mr. Dooley's Philosophy, 1900

Vice is a creature of such hideous mien that the more you see it the better you like it.

Mr. Dooley's Opinions, 1901

LORD DUNSANY
1878–1957   Irish dramatist and short-story writer

Humanity, let us say, is like people packed in an automobile which is travelling downhill without lights at terrific speed and driven by a small four-year-old child. The signposts along the way are all marked 'Progress'.

in 1954

KAREN DURBIN
1944–   American writer

Marriage is two people agreeing to tell the same lie.

LEO DUROCHER
1906–   American baseball manager

Show me a good loser in professional sports and I'll show you an idiot. Show me a good sportsman and I'll show you a player I'm looking to trade.

1950

LAWRENCE DURRELL
1912–   British writer

History is an endless repetition of the wrong way of living.

The Listener, 1978

IAN DURY
1943–   British rock composer and singer

The hope that springs eternal
Springs right up your behind.

'This Is What We Find', 1979

WALTER DWIGHT

1872–1923   American clergyman

Politicians speak for their parties, and parties never are, never have been and never will be wrong.

ABBA EBAN
1915–   Israeli politician

History teaches us that men and nations behave wisely once they have exhausted all other alternatives.

in 1970

Propaganda is the art of persuading others of what one does not believe oneself.

PAUL EHRLICH
1854–1915   American scientist

The mother of the year should be a sterilized woman with two adopted children.

PAUL ELDRIDGE
1888–?   American writer

The nearest approach to immortality for any truth is by its becoming a platitude.

Horns of Glass, 1943

GEORGE ELIOT (Mary Ann Evans)
1819–1880   British novelist

I'm not denyin' the women are foolish: God Almighty made 'em to match the men.

Adam Bede, 1859

T. S. ELIOT

1888–1965   American-born British poet

Immature poets imitate, mature poets steal.

'Philip Massinger', 1920

So far as we are human, what we do must be either evil or good: so far as we do evil or good, we are human: and it is better, in a paradoxical way, to do evil than to do nothing: at least we exist.

essay on Baudelaire

Success is relative:
It is what we can make of the mess we have made of things.

The Family Reunion, 1939

HAVELOCK ELLIS

1859–1939   British sexologist

What we call 'progress' is the exchange of one nuisance for another nuisance.

The whole religious complexion of the modern world is due to the absence from Jerusalem of a lunatic asylum.

RALPH WALDO EMERSON

1803–1882   American essayist, poet and philosopher

The louder he talked of his honour, the faster we counted our spoons.

A sect or party is an elegant incognito devised to save a man from the vexation of thinking.

Journals, 1831

The hater of property and of government takes care to have his warranty deed recorded, and the book written against fame and learning has the author's name on the title page.

Ibid.

Democracy becomes a government of bullies, tempered by editors.

NORA EPHRON
1941– American writer

If pregnancy were a book they would cut the last two chapters.
Heartburn, 198[

DESIDERIUS ERASMUS
1466–1536 Dutch humanist

War is delightful to those who have had no experience of it.

SUSAN ERTZ
American writer

Millions long for immortality who do not know what to do with
themselves on a rainy Sunday afternoon.
quoted in *Quotations for Speakers and Writers*, ed. A. Andrew

EVAN ESAR
1899– American writer

A gentleman is a man who wouldn't hit a lady with his hat on.

The girl with a future avoids the man with a past.
The Humor of Humor, 195

BERGAN EVANS
1904– American educator

Lying is an indispensable part of making life tolerable.

HAROLD EVANS
1928– British journalist

The camera cannot lie. But it can be an accessory to untruth.
Pictures on a Page, 197

BOB EZRIN
American rock music producer

The key to building a superstar is to keep their mouth shut. To reveal an artist to the people can be to destroy him. It isn't to anyone's advantage to see the truth.

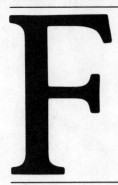F

CLIFTON FADIMAN
1904– American essayist

We prefer to believe that the absence of inverted commas guarantees the originality of a thought, whereas it may be merely that the utterer has forgotten its source.

Any Number Can Play, 1957

Experience teaches you that the man who looks you straight in the eye, particularly if he adds a firm handshake, is hiding something.

Enter, Conversing

For most men life is a search for the proper manila envelope in which to get themselves filed.

1960

WILLIAM FAULKNER
1897–1962 American novelist

A writer is congenitally unable to tell the truth and that is why we call what he writes fiction.

quoted in his obituary, 1962

JAMES K. FEIBLEMAN
1904– American philospher

A myth is a religion in which no-one any longer believes.

Understanding Philosophy, 1973

JULES FEIFFER
1929– American cartoonist

The big mistake that men make is that when they turn thirteen or fourteen and all of a sudden they've reached puberty, they believe that they like women. Actually, you're just horny. It doesn't mean you like women any more at twenty-one than you did at ten.

quoted in Loose Talk, ed. L. Botts, 1980

Christ died for our sins. Dare we make his martyrdom meaningless by not committing them?

quoted in Peter's Quotations, ed. L. Peter, 1977

EDNA FERBER
1887–1968 American writer

A woman can look both moral and exciting – if she also looks as if it were quite a struggle.

Reader's Digest, 1954

HENRY FIELDING
1707–1754 British novelist

His designs were strictly honourable, as the phrase is: that is, to rob a lady of her fortune by way of marriage.

Tom Jones, 1749

A generous man is merely a fool in the eyes of a thief.

Ibid.

W. C. FIELDS
1879–1946 American film star

Women are like elephants to me: I like to look at them, but I wouldn't want to own one.

never vote for anyone. I always vote against.

FINAGLE'S LAWS

First Law: if an experiment works, something has gone wrong.
Fourth Law: once a job is fouled up, anything done to improve it only makes it worse.

> quoted in *Murphy's Law* by A. Bloch, 1979

FIRST LAW OF DEBATE

Never argue with a fool – people might not know the difference.

> *Ibid.*

F. SCOTT FITZGERALD
1896–1940   American writer

One girl can be pretty – but a dozen are only a chorus.

> *The Last Tycoon*, 1941

Optimism is the content of small men in high places.

> *The Crack Up*, 1945

GUSTAVE FLAUBERT
1821–1880   French novelist

What is glory? It is to have a lot of nonsense talked about you.

> quoted in *A Cynic's Breviary* by J. R. Solly, 1925

ROBERT DE FLERS
1872–1927   French playwright

Democracy is the name we give to the people each time we need them

> *L'Habit vert*, 1912

HENRY FORD
1863–1947   American industrialist

An idealist is one who helps the other fellow to make a profit.

E. M. FORSTER
1879–1970   British writer

There lies at the back of every creed something terrible and hard for which the worshipper may one day be required to suffer.
Two Cheers for Democracy, 1951

THE FOUR-F CLUB

Find 'em, feel 'em, fuck 'em and forget 'em.
motto of 1950s teenage males

CHARLES JAMES FOX
1749–1806   British statesman

Kings govern by means of popular assemblies only when they cannot do without them.

1776

JANET FRAME
1924–   New Zealand writer

'For your own good' is a persuasive argument that will eventually make a man agree to his own destruction.
Faces in the Water

ANATOLE FRANCE (Jacques Anatole Thibault)
1844–1924   French novelist, poet and critic

It is in the ability to deceive oneself that one shows the greatest talent.

It is only the poor who pay cash, and that not from virtue, but because they are refused credit.
quoted in *A Cynic's Breviary* by J. R. Solly, 1925

Justice is the sanction of established injustice.
Crainquebille, 1901

Christianity has done love a great service by making it a sin.
The Garden of Epicurus, 1894

The law, in all its majestic equality, forbids the rich as well as the poor to sleep under bridges.

BRENDAN FRANCIS

The big difference between sex for money and sex for free is that sex for money usually costs a lot less.

What a man enjoys about a woman's clothes are his fantasies of how she would look without them.

Politicians, like prostitutes, are held in contempt. But what man does not run to them when he needs their services?

What an author likes to write most is his signature on the back of a cheque.

Many a man has decided to stay alive not because of the will to live, but because of the determination not to give assorted surviving bastards the satisfaction of his death.

Most people perform essentially meaningless work. When they retire that truth is borne in upon them.

BENJAMIN FRANKLIN
1706–1790   American scientist and statesman

Many a long dispute between divines may thus be abridged: It is so. It is not so. It is so. It is not so.

Poor Richard's Almanack, 1743

In this world, nothing is certain but death and taxes.

1789

All would live long, but none would be old.

He that teaches himself has a fool for a master.

Love your neighbour, yet don't pull down your hedge.

SIGMUND FREUD
1856–1939   Austrian psychoanalyst

The credulity of love is the most fundamental source of authority.

Collected Works, 1955

EDGAR Z. FRIEDENBERG
1921–   American sociologist

It takes a kind of shabby arrogance to survive in our time, and a fairly romantic nature to want to.

The Vanishing Adolescent, 1959

Romance, like alcohol, should be enjoyed, but should not be allowed to become necessary.

Ibid.

Not only do people accept violence if it is perpetrated by legitimate authority, they also regard violence against certain kinds of people as inherently legitimate, no matter who commits it.

1966

BRUCE J. FRIEDMAN
1930–   American writer

A Code of Honour: never approach a friend's girlfriend or wife with mischief as your goal. There are too many women in the world to justify that sort of dishonourable behaviour. Unless she's really attractive.

Sex and the Lonely Guy, 1977

MILTON FRIEDMAN
1912–   American economist

There's no such thing as a free lunch.

One man's opportunism is another man's statesmanship.

Playboy magazine, 1973

Governments never learn. Only people learn.

quoted 1980

DAVID FROST
1939– British television personality

Television is an invention that permits you to be entertained in your living room by people you wouldn't have in your home.

on CBS-TV, 1971

ROBERT FROST
1874–1963 American poet

A jury consists of twelve persons chosen to decide who has the better lawyer.

A liberal is a man too broadminded to take his own side in a quarrel.

If society fits you comfortably enough, you call it freedom.

Esquire magazine, 1965

A bank is a place where they lend you an umbrella in fair weather and ask for it back when it begins to rain.

Home is the place where, when you have to go there, they have to take you in.

DOROTHY FULDHEIM
1893– American writer

Youth is a disease from which we all recover.

A Thousand Friends, 1974

BUCKMINSTER FULLER
1895–1983 American architect and inventor

Faith is much better than belief. Belief is when someone else does the thinking.

Playboy magazine. 1972

G. RAY FUNKHOUSER

The quality of legislation passed to deal with a problem is inversely proportional to the volume of media clamour that brought it on.

quoted in *The Official Rules* by P. Dickson, 1978

ZSA ZSA GABOR
1919–   Hungarian film star

A man in love is incomplete until he is married. Then he is finished.
Newsweek magazine, 1960

JOHN KENNETH GALBRAITH
1908–   American economist

The salary of the chief executive of the large corporation is not a
market award for achievement. It is frequently in the nature of a
warm personal gesture by the individual to himself.
Annals of an Abiding Liberal, 1980

Meetings are indispensable when you don't want to do anything.
Ambassador's Journal, 1969

Politics is not the art of the possible. It consists in choosing between
the disastrous and the unpalatable.

1969

There is an insistent tendency among serious social scientists to think
of any institution which features rhymed and singing commercials,
intense and lachrymose voices urging highly improbable enjoyment,
caricatures of the human oesophagus in normal or impaired operation,
and which hints implausibly at opportunities for antiseptic seduction
as inherently trivial. This is a great mistake. The industrial system is
profoundly dependent on commercial television and could not exist
in its present form without it.
The New Industrial State, 1967

What is called a high standard of living, consists in considerable
measure, in arrangements for avoiding muscular energy, increasing
sensual pleasure, enhancing caloric intake beyond any conceivable

79

nutritional requirement. Nonetheless, the belief that increased production is a worthy social goal is very nearly absolute.

Ibid.

Few things are as immutable as the addiction of political groups to the ideas by which they have once won office.

The Affluent Society, 1958

Anyone who says he isn't going to resign, four times, definitely will.

Nothing is so admirable in politics as a short memory.

PIERRE GALLOIS
1911–   French scientist

If you put tomfoolery into a computer, nothing comes out but tomfoolery. But this tomfoolery, having passed through a very expensive machine, is somehow ennobled and no-one dares criticise it.

quoted in *Reader's Digest*

JOHN GALSWORTHY
1867–1933   British novelist and playwright

There's just one rule for politicians all over the world. Don't say in power what you say in opposition. If you do, you'll only have to carry out what the other fellows have found impossible.

Maids in Waiting, 1931

Idealism increases in direct proportion to one's distance from the problem.

CHRIS GARRATT and MICK KIDD
British cartoonists

Life is a meaningless comma in the sentence of time.

The Essential Biff, 1982

PAUL GAUGUIN
1848–1903   French painter

Life being what it is, one dreams of revenge.

JOHN GAY
1685–1732   British playwright

The comfortable estate of widowhood is the only hope that keeps up a wife's spirits.

The Beggar's Opera, 1728

JEAN GENET
1910–   French playwright

Crimes of which a people is ashamed constitute its real history. The same is true of man.

notes for *The Screens*, 1973

DAVID GERROLD
1944–   American science fiction writer

The human race never solves any of its problems. It merely outlives them.

Starlog magazine, 1978

EDWARD GIBBON
1737–1794   British historian

Corruption . . . the most infallible symptom of constitutional liberty.

GEORGE GIBBS
1870–1942

I think it can be stated without denial that no man ever saw a man he would be willing to marry if he were a woman.

How to Stay Married, 1925

WOLCOTT GIBBS
1902–1958   American critic

Generally speaking, the . . . theatre is the aspirin of the middle classes.

More in Sorrow, 1958

GINSBERG'S THEOREM

1. You can't win. 2. You can't break even. 3. You can't even quit the game.

quoted in Murphy's Law by A. Bloch, 1979

JEAN GIRAUDOUX
1882–1944   French playwright

There is no better way of exercising the imagination than the study of law. No poet ever interpreted nature as freely as a lawyer interprets truth.

Tiger at the Gates, 1935

To win a woman in the first place one must please her, then undress her, and then somehow get her clothes back on her. Finally, so she will allow you to leave her, you've got to annoy her.

Amphitryon 38, 1929

The secret of success is sincerity. Once you can fake that you've got it made.

quoted in Murphy's Law Book Two by A. Bloch, 1980

HERMANN GOERING
1893–1945   German Reichsmarschall

If you really want to do something new, the good won't help you with it. Let me have men about me that are arrant knaves. The wicked, who have something on their conscience, are obliging, quick to hear threats, because they know how it's done, and for booty. You can offer them things because they will take them. Because they have no hesitations. You can hang them if they get out of step. Let me have men about me that are utter villains – provided that I have the power, the absolute power, over life and death.

If people say that here and there someone has been taken away and maltreated, I can only reply: You can't make an omelette without breaking eggs.

1933

Naturally the common people don't want war . . . but after all it is the leaders of a country who determine policy, and it is always a simple matter to drag the people along, whether it is a democracy, or a fascist dictatorship, or a parliament or a communist dictatorship. All you have to do is tell them they are being attacked, and denounce the pacifists for lack of patriotism and exposing the country to danger. It works the same in every country.

> quoted in *The People's Almanac*, 1976

JOHANN WOLFGANG VON GOETHE
1749–1832   German poet

Love is an ideal thing, marriage a real thing; a confusion of the real with the ideal never goes unpunished.

For the butterfly, mating and propagation involve the sacrifice of life, for the human being, the sacrifice of beauty.

He who cannot love must learn to flatter.

In politics, as on the sickbed, people toss from side to side, thinking they will be more comfortable.

CARLO GOLDONI
1707–1793   Italian playwright

The blush is beautiful, but sometimes it is inconvenient.

OLIVER GOLDSMITH
1728–1774   British poet and playwright

Nothing can exceed the vanity of our existence but the folly of our pursuits.

> *The Good-Natured Man*, 1768

Friendship is a disinterested commerce between equals; love, an abject intercourse between tyrants and slaves.

> *Ibid.*

There is nothing so absurd or ridiculous that has not at some time been said by some philosopher.

EDMOND DE GONCOURT
1822–1896   French diarist

Genius is the talent of a man who is dead.

PAUL GOODMAN
1911–1972   American educator and writer

When there is official censorship it is a sign that speech is serious.
When there is none, it is pretty certain that the official spokesmen
have all the loudspeakers.

Growing Up Absurd, 1960

The organisation of American society is an interlocking system of
semi-monopolies notoriously venal, an electorate notoriously
unenlightened, misled by a mass media notoriously phoney.

The Community of Scholars, 1962

REMY DE GOURMONT
1858–1910   French writer and philosopher

Of all the sexual aberrations, perhaps the most peculiar is chastity.

BALTASAR GRACIAN
1601–1658   Spanish writer

A beautiful woman should break her mirror early.

The truest wild beasts live in the most populous places.

The Art of Worldly Wisdom, 1647

Everything is good or everything is bad, according to the votes they
gain.

Ibid.

GRAFFITI

God is not dead. He is alive and working on a much less ambitious
project.

London, 1975

If voting changed anything, they'd make it illegal.

London, 1979

We are the unwilling, led by the unqualified, doing the unnecessary for
the ungrateful.

Vietnam, 1960s, 1970s

Death is life's answer to the question 'Why?'

Death is nature's way of telling you to slow down.

The only difference between graffiti and philosophy is the word 'fuck'.

Life is a hereditary disease.

God is alive, he just doesn't want to get involved.

Everything starts as a mystique and ends as politics.

Paris, 1968

If you can keep your head when all about you are losing theirs,
perhaps you have misunderstood the situation.

GÜNTER GRASS
1927–   German writer and politician

Never sleep three in a bed – or you'll wake up three in a bed.

Dog Years, 1966

THE GREEN BERETS

If you've got them by the balls, their hearts and minds will follow.

military motto

GRAHAM GREENE
1904–   British novelist

Heresy is only another word for freedom of thought.

quoted 1981

Sentimentality – that's what we call the sentiment we don't share.

quoted in *Quotations for Speakers and Writers*, ed. A. Andrews

GERMAINE GREER
1939–   Australian feminist

Probably the only place where a man can feel really secure is in a
maximum security prison, except for the imminent threat of release.

The Female Eunuch, 1970

Mother is the dead heart of the family, spending father's earnings on consumer goods to enhance the environment in which he eats, sleeps and watches the television.

Ibid.

Love, love, love – all the wretched cant of it, masking egotism, lust, masochism, fantasy under a mythology of sentimental postures, a welter of self-induced miseries and joys, blinding and masking the essential personalities in the frozen gestures of courtship, in the kissing and the dating and the desire, the compliments and the quarrels which vivify its barrenness.

Ibid.

DICK GREGORY
1932–   American comedian

Hell hath no fury like a liberal scorned.

JOHN GRIGG
1924–   British writer

It is no part of the State's duty to facilitate the spiritual redemption of rich men by impoverishing them in this life.

1964

WHITNEY GRISWOLD
1909–1963   American academic

Things have got to be wrong in order that they may be deplored.
quoted in the *New York Times*, 1963

WALTER GROPIUS
1883–1969   German architect

Specialists are people who always repeat the same mistakes.
quoted in *Contemporary Architects*, 1980

PHILIP GUEDALLA
1889–1944   British writer

Autobiography is an unrivalled vehicle for telling the truth about other people.

SACHA GUITRY
1885–1957   French actor and playwright

The most important thing in life is not to have money, but that others have it.

Le Scandale de Monte Carlo

When a man steals your wife, there is no better revenge than to let him keep her.

Elles et toi, 1948

GYP (Comtesse de Martel de Janville)
1850–1932   French novelist

The woman who does not marry makes a blunder that can only be compared to that of the man who does.

quoted in *A Cynic's Breviary* by J. R. Solly, 1925

We don't ask others to be faultless, we only ask that their faults should not incommode our own.

Ibid.

GEORGE SAVILE, MARQUIS OF HALIFAX
1633–1695 British author and politician

Men who borrow their opinions can never repay their debts.

Miscellaneous Thoughts and Reflections

If the commending others did not recommend ourselves, there would be few panegyrics.

Ibid.

When the people contend for their liberty they seldom get anything for their victory but new masters.

The best Party is but a kind of conspiracy against the rest of the nation ... Ignorance maketh men go into a party, and shame keepeth them from going out of it.

MARGARET HALSEY
1910– American writer

The attitude of the English towards English history reminds one a good deal of the attitude of a Hollywood director towards love.

With Malice Toward Some

The English never smash in a face. They merely refrain from asking it to dinner.

Ibid.

PERCY HAMMOND
1873–1936   American critic

The more you do for an actor the worse it hates you.
quoted in *Selected Letters of James Thurber*,
ed. H. Thurber and E. Weeks, 1981

LAING HANCOCK
1909–   Australian industrialist

The best way to help the poor is not to become one of them.
The Bulletin magazine, 1977

JUDGE LEARNED HAND
1872–1961   American jurist

Liberty is so much latitude as the powerful choose to accord to the weak.

quoted 1930

RICHARD HARKNESS

What is a committee? A group of the unwilling, picked from the unfit, to do the unnecessary.
quoted in the *New York Herald Tribune*, 1960

SYDNEY J. HARRIS
1917–   American journalist

Any philosophy that can be put 'in a nutshell' belongs there.
Leaving the Surface, 1968

A cynic is not merely one who reads bitter lessons from the past, he is one who is prematurely disappointed in the future.
On the Contrary, 1962

You may be sure that when a man begins to call himself a realist he is preparing to do something that he is secretly ashamed of doing.

HENRY HASKINS
b. 1875   American writer

The voyage of love is all the sweeter for an outside stateroom and a seat at the Captain's table.

Meditations in Wall Street, 1940

Hope must feel that the human breast is amazingly tolerant.

Ibid.

JOHN W. HAZARD
1912–

Gumperson's Law: the probability of anything happening is in inverse ratio to its desirability.

Changing Times, 1957

WILLIAM HAZLITT
1778–1830   British essayist

It is essential to the triumph of reform that it should never succeed.

We are not satisfied to be right, unless we can prove others to be quite wrong.

BEN HECHT
1894–1964   American journalist and screenwriter

A man in love, like Romeo, can no more join his beloved between the sheets than push his dear mother off a roof, at least, not for some time.

Letters from Bohemia

Love is a hole in the heart.

Winkelberg, 1950

GEORG WILHELM FRIEDRICH HEGEL
1770–1831   German philosopher

The people are that part of the state which does not know what it wants.

We learn from history that we do not learn from history.

HEINRICH HEINE
1797–1856   German poet

The music at a wedding procession always reminds me of the music of soldiers going into battle.

One should forgive one's enemies, but not before they are hanged.

JOSEPH HELLER
1923–   American novelist

Success and failure are both difficult to endure. Along with success come drugs, divorce, fornication, bullying, travel, meditation, medication, depression, neurosis and suicide. With failure comes failure.

Playboy magazine, 1975

Some men are born mediocre, some men achieve mediocrity, and some men have mediocrity thrust upon them.

ROBERT HELLER
1919–   American writer

The first myth of management is that it exists. The second myth of management is that success equals skill.

The Great Executive Dream, 1972

SIR ARTHUR HELPS
1813–1875   British author

The greatest luxury of riches is, that they enable you to escape so much good advice.

It is an error to suppose that no man understands his own character. Most persons know even their failings very well, only they persist in giving them names different from those usually assigned by the rest of the world.

Thoughts in the Cloister and the Crowd, 1835

ERNEST HEMINGWAY
1899–1961   American writer

Love is something that hangs up behind the bathroom door and smells of Lysol.

To Have and Have Not, 1937

People who write fiction, if they had not taken it up, might have become very successful liars.

This Week, 1959

If two people love each other, there can be no happy end to it.

DONAL HENAHAN
American writer

Next to the writer of real estate advertisements, the autobiographer is the most suspect of prose artists.

New York Times, 1977

OLIVER HERFORD
1863–1935   American writer

Darling: the popular form of address used in speaking to a member of the opposite sex whose name you cannot at the moment remember.

Liar: one who tells an unpleasant truth.

Modesty: the gentle art of enhancing your charm by pretending not to be aware of it.

OLIVER HERFORD and JOHN C. CLAY
Adam's Rib: the original bone of contention.

Cupid's Cyclopaedia, 1910

Blush: a weakness of youth and an accomplishment of experience.

Ibid.

Cash: a sort of window-fastener to keep Love from flying out.

Ibid.

Dream: fem. a term used by a woman discussing a hat; masc. term describing the woman used by the man who is destined to buy the hat.

Ibid.

Marriage: the conventional ending of a love affair. A lonesome state.

Ibid.

Wedding: a necessary formality before securing a divorce.

Ibid.

HERODOTUS
484?–425 BC   Greek historian

Very few things happen at the right time, and the rest do not happen at all. The conscientious historian will correct these defects.

DON HEROLD
b. 1889   American humorist

Poverty must have its satisfactions, else there would not be so many poor people.

ALEXANDER HERZEN
1812–1870   Russian political theorist

History is the autobiography of a madman.

Dr. Krupov

SIR SEYMOUR HICKS
1871–1949   British actor

A man does not buy his wife a fur coat to keep her warm, but to keep her pleasant.

Observer, 1946

BENNY HILL
1925–   British comedian

That's what show business is – sincere insincerity.

Observer, 1977

ADOLF HITLER
1889–1945   German dictator

commenting on exceptionally heavy casualty lists:

But then, that's what young men are there for.

What luck for the rulers that men do not think.

Everlasting peace will come to the world when the last man has slain the last but one.

I shall give a propagandist reason for starting the war, no matter whether it is plausible or not. The victor will not be asked afterwards whether he told the truth or not. When starting and waging war it is not right that matters, but victory.

THOMAS HOBBES
1588–1679   British political theorist

Laughter is nothing else but sudden glory arising from some sudden conception of some eminency in ourselves, by comparison with the infirmity of others, or with our own formerly.

On Human Nature, 1650

During the time men live without a common power to keep them all in awe, . . . the life of man [is] solitary, poor, nasty, brutish and short.

Leviathan, 1651

So that in the first place I put for a general inclination of all mankind a perpetual and restless desire of power after power, that ceases only in death.

Ibid.

DAVID HOCKNEY
1937–   British artist

It is very good advice to believe only what an artist does, rather than what he says about his work.

David Hockney, 1976

SAMUEL HOFFENSTEIN
1890–1947   American poet

When you're away, I'm restless, lonely
Wretched, bored, dejected, only
Here's the rub, my darling dear,
I feel the same when you are here.
                    Poems in Praise of Practically Nothing, 1929

ERIC HOFFER
1902–   American philosopher

When people are free to do as they please, they usually imitate each
other.
                    The Passionate State of Mind, 1954

DUSTIN HOFFMAN
1937–   American film star

A good review from the critics is just another stay of execution.
                    Playboy magazine, 1975

RICHARD HOFSTADTER
1916–1970   American historian

Yesterday's avant-garde experience is today's chic and tomorrow's
cliché.
                    Anti-Intellectualism in American Life, 1963

FRIEDRICH HÖLDERLIN
1770–1843   German poet

What has always made the state a hell on earth has been precisely that
man has tried to make it his heaven.

OLIVER WENDELL HOLMES, Sr.
1809–1894   American man of letters and jurist

Apology is only egotism wrong side out.

Fresh air and innocence are good if you don't take too much of them

ANTHONY HOPE (Sir Anthony Hope Hawkins)
1863–1933   British writer

Unless one is a genius, it is best to aim at being intelligible.

The Dolly Dialogues, 1894

HEDDA HOPPER
1890–1966   Hollywood gossip columnist

Nobody's interested in sweetness and light.

EDGAR WATSON HOWE
1853–1937   American writer

Marriage is a good deal like a circus: there is not as much in it as is represented in the advertising.

Country Town Sayings, 1911

ELBERT HUBBARD
1856–1915   American writer and businessman

The selfish wish to govern is often mistaken for a holy zeal in the cause of humanity.

The Notebook, 1927

A creed is an ossified metaphor.

Ibid.

A conservative is a man who is too cowardly to fight and too fat to run.

Ibid.

A pessimist is a man who has been compelled to live with an optimist.

Ibid.

Heaven: the Coney Island of the Christian imagination.

Ibid.

KIN HUBBARD (Frank McKinney Hubbard)
1868–1930   American humorist

Classical music is the kind we keep thinking will turn into a tune.

Abe Martin's Sayings, 1915

Just because a girl's married ain't no sign she hasn't loved and lost.
Abe Martin on Things in General

Boys will be boys, and so will a lot of middle-aged men.

After a girl gets too big for Santa Claus, she begins to cast around for an easy mark.
Abe Martin's Primer

Nobody ever forgets where he buried the hatchet.

The less a statesman amounts to, the more he loves the flag.

DAVID HUME
1711–1766 Scottish political theorist

Nothing appears more surprising to those who consider human affairs with a philosophical eye, than the ease with which the many are governed by the few.
The First Principles of Government, 1742

JAMES GIBBONS HUNEKER
1860–1921 American writer

Life is like an onion: you peel off layer after layer and then you find there is nothing in it.

JACK HURLEY
American boxing manager

Every young man should have a hobby: learning how to handle money is the best one.
1961

ROBERT M. HUTCHINS
b. 1899 American academic

The death of democracy is not likely to be assassination from ambush. It will be a slow extinction from apathy, indifference and under-nourishment.

ALDOUS HUXLEY
1894–1963   British writer

A man may have strong humanitarian and democratic principles, but if he happens to have been brought up as a bath-taking, shirt-changing lover of fresh air, he will have to overcome certain physical repugnances before he can bring himself to put these principles into practice.

Jesting Pilate, 1926

The word 'love' bridges for us those chasms of momentary indifference and boredom which gape from time to time between even the most ardent lovers.

The Olive Tree, 1937

Only one more indispensable massacre of Capitalists or Communists or Fascists or Christians or Heretics and there we are – there we are in the Golden Future.

Time Must Have a Stop, 1944

As long as men worship the Caesars and Napoleons, the Caesars and Napoleons will duly rise and make them miserable.

Ends and Means, 1937

That men do not learn very much from history is the most important of all the lessons that history has to teach.

Collected Essays, 1959

The most distressing thing that can happen to a prophet is to be proved wrong. The next most distressing thing is to be proved right.

Brave New World Revisited, 1956

Idealism is the noble toga that political gentlemen drape over their will to power.

1963

T. H. HUXLEY
1825–1895   British scientist

A man's worst difficulties begin when he is able to do as he likes.

HENRIK IBSEN
1828–1906 Norwegian playwright

Do not use that foreign word 'ideals'. We have that excellent native
word 'lies'.

The Wild Duck, 1884

WILLIAM R. INGE
1860–1954 British clergyman

Many people believe they are attracted by God, or by Nature, when
they are only repelled by man.

More Lay Thoughts of a Dean, 1931

Originality is undetected plagiarism.

Universal suffrage almost inevitably leads to government by mass
bribery, an auction of the wordly goods of the unrepresented
minority.

ROBERT G. INGERSOLL
1833–1899 American lawyer and agnostic

In all ages hypocrites, called priests, have put crowns on the heads of
thieves, called kings.

1884

EUGÈNE IONESCO
1912– Romanian-born French playwright

To think contrary to one's era is heroism. But to speak against it is
madness.

In the name of religion, one tortures, persecutes, builds pyres. In the guise of ideologies, one massacres, tortures and kills. In the name of justice one punishes . . . in the name of love of one's country or of one's race one hates other countries, despises them, massacres them. In the name of equality and brotherhood there is suppression and torture. There is nothing in common between the means and the end, the means go far beyond the end . . . ideologies and religion . . . are the alibis of the means.

Esquire magazine, 1974

WASHINGTON IRVING
1783–1859   American diplomat and author

A sharp tongue is the only edged instrument that grows keener with constant use.

The Sketch Book, 1820

For what is history but a kind of Newgate Calendar, a register of the crimes and miseries that man has inflicted on his fellow men? It is a huge libel on human nature.

History of New York, 1809

ITALIAN PROVERB
What you can't have, abuse.

HOLBROOK JACKSON
1874–1948 British writer

Why did nature create Man? Was it to show that she is big enough to make mistakes, or was it pure ignorance?

WILLIAM JAMES
1842–1910 American philosopher

A great many people think they are thinking when they are merely rearranging their prejudices.

PIERRE JANET
1859–1947 French psychiatrist

If a patient is poor he is committed to a public hospital as a 'psychotic'. If he can afford a sanatorium, the diagnosis is 'neurasthenia'. If he is wealthy enough to be in his own home under the constant watch of nurses and physicians, he is simply 'an indisposed eccentric'.
quoted in The Wit of Medicine, ed. L. and M. Cowan, 1972

ROGER JELLINEK
American writer

The purpose of Presidential office is not power, or leadership of the Western world, but reminiscence, best-selling reminiscence.
New York Times Book Review, 1969

ELIZABETH JENKINS
British writer

The woman whose behaviour indicates that she will make a scene if she is told the truth asks to be deceived.

quoted in *The Faber Book of Aphorisms*,
ed. Auden and Kronenberger, 1964

JEROME K. JEROME
1859–1927   British humorist

It is always the best policy to tell the truth, unless, of course, you are an exceptionally good liar.

SIR GEORGE JESSEL
1891–1977   British politician

The human brain starts working the moment you are born and never stops until you stand up to speak in public.

1949

DR SAMUEL JOHNSON
1709–1784   British critic, poet and lexicographer

A gentleman who had been very unhappy in marriage married immediately after his wife died: Johnson said it was the triumph of hope over experience.

The Life of Samuel Johnson by James Boswell, 1791

The advice that is wanted is commonly unwelcome, and that which is not wanted is evidently impertinent.

The Piozzi Letters, 1788

There is no kind of idleness by which we are so easily seduced as that which dignifies itself by the appearance of business.

The Idler, 1758

No man but a blockhead ever wrote except for money.

The Life of Samuel Johnson by James Boswell, 1791

Such is the state of life, that none are happy but by the anticipation of change: the change itself is nothing; when we have made it the next wish is to change again.

Rasselas, 1759

Is not a Patron . . . one who looks with unconcern on a man struggling for life in the water, and, when he has reached ground, encumbers him with help?

The Life of Samuel Johnson by James Boswell, 1791

To find a new country and invade it has always been the same thing.

Works V

Distance either of time or place is sufficient to reconcile weak minds to wonderful relations.

Ibid.

Honesty is not greater where elegance is less.

Works IX

Pointed axioms and acute replies fly loose about the world, and are assigned successively to those whom it may be the fashion to celebrate.

Works VII

Pride is a vice which pride itself inclines every man to find in others and to overlook in himself.

Works VI

We are inclined to believe those whom we do not know because they have never deceived us.

The Idler, 1758

Those whom their virtue restrains from deceiving others are often disposed by their vanity to deceive themselves.

Works VIII

That the vulgar express their thoughts clearly is far from true; and what perspicuity can be found among them proceeds not from the easiness of their language, but the shallowness of their thoughts.

The Idler, 1758

Be not too hasty to trust or admire the teachers of morality: they discourse like angels but they live like men.

Rasselas, 1759

About things on which the public thinks long, it commonly attains to think right.

Works VII

A man had rather have a hundred lies told of him, than one truth which he does not wish should be told.
                                    The Life of Samuel Johnson by James Boswell, 1791

answering the query 'I wonder what pleasure men can take in making beasts of themselves?':

He who makes a beast of himself gets rid of the pain of being a man.
                                    Murray's Johnsoniana

Human life is everywhere a state in which much is to be endured and little to be enjoyed.
                                    Rasselas, 1759

We are to consider mankind not as we wish them, but as we find them, frequently corrupt and always fallible.
                                    Works XI

The history of mankind is little else than a narrative of designs which have failed, and hopes that have been disappointed.
                                    Works IX

Depend upon it that if a man talks of his misfortunes, there is something in them that is not disagreeable to him.
                                    The Life of Samuel Johnson by James Boswell, 1791

The whole of life is but keeping away the thoughts of death.
                                    Ibid.

Patriotism is the last refuge of a scoundrel. (cf. R. Conkling)
                                    Ibid.

Politics are . . . nothing more than a means of rising in the world.
                                    1775

There are few minds to which tyranny is not delightful.

I would not give half a guinea to live under one form of government rather than another. It is of no moment to the happiness of an individual.
                                    1772

ALVA JOHNSTON
d. 1950   American writer

The title 'Little Napoleon' in Hollywood is equivalent to the title 'Mister' in any other community.

BEVERLY JONES
1927– American feminist

Romance, like the rabbit at the dog track, is the elusive, fake, and never attained reward which, for the benefit and amusement of our masters, keeps us running and thinking in safe circles.
The Florida Paper on Women's Liberation, 1970

SIR ELWYN JONES
1904– British lawyer

Someone has described a technicality as a point of principle which we have forgotten.

1966

FRANKLIN P. JONES

Experience enables you to recognise a mistake when you make it again.

JAMES JONES
1921– American novelist

Conversation is more often likely to be an attempt at deliberate evasion, deliberate confusion, rather than communication. We are all cheats and liars, really.
Writers at Work, 3rd series, 1957

SIR WILLIAM JONES

My opinion is that power should be distrusted, in whatever hands it is based.

1782

JONES' LAW

The man who smiles when things go wrong has thought of someone he can blame it on.
quoted in *Murphy's Law* by A. Bloch, 1979

BEN JONSON
1573–1637   British poet and playwright

They say princes learn no art truly, but the art of horsemanship. The reason is, the brave beast is no flatterer. He will throw a prince as soon as his groom.

Timber; or Discoveries, 164(

MICHAEL JOSEPH
1897–1958   British publisher

Authors are easy to get on with – if you're fond of children.

Observer, 194%

ERIC JULBER
American lawyer

One should be suspicious of 'love' as a political slogan. A government which purports to 'love' its citizens invariably desires all the prerogatives of a lover: to share the loved one's thoughts and to keep him in bondage.

Esquire magazine, 196%

C. G. JUNG
1875–1961   Austrian psychoanalyst

Sentimentality is a superstructure covering brutality.

Reflections, 195:

JUVENAL (Decimus Junius Juvenalis)
60?–?140   Roman satirist

For women's tears are but the sweat of eyes

Satire

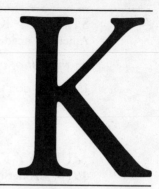

FRANZ KAFKA
1883–1924   Czech writer

Every revolution evaporates and leaves behind only the slime of a new bureaucracy.

The meaning of life is that it stops.

ALPHONSE KARR
1808–1890   French journalist and novelist

Many people think that virtue consists of severity towards others.
quoted in *A Cynic's Breviary* by J. R. Solly, 1925

GEORGE S. KAUFMAN
1889–1961   American playwright

theatrical dictum:

Satire is what closes Saturday night.

EMERY KELEN
b. 1896   American journalist

The interview is an intimate conversation between journalist and politician wherein the journalist seeks to take advantage of the garrulity of the politician and the politician of the credulity of the journalist.

STANLEY KELLEY
American academic

on the cult of victory at all costs:

Last guys don't finish nice.

> quoted in *The Official Rules* by P. Dickson, 1978

MURRAY KEMPTON
1917–   American journalist

It is a function of government to invent philosophies to explain the demands of its own convenience.

> *America Comes of Middle Age*, 1963

A revolution requires of its leaders a record of unbroken infallibility. If they do not possess it they are expected to invent it.

> *Part of Our Time*, 1955

The general law of development for political institutions conceived in revolutionary idealism, which is that they begin as an expression of conscience and become in due course agencies for the issuance of licences and the distribution of patronage.

> *Newsday* magazine, 1981

A man can look upon his life and accept it as good or evil; it is far, far harder for him to confess that it has been unimportant in the sum of things.

> *Part of Our Time*, 1955

FRANK KENT
1907?–1978   American journalist

The only way a reporter should look at a politician is down.

> quoted in *The Boys on the Bus* by T. Crouse, 1973

CHARLES F. KETTERING
1876–1958   American businessman

The difference between intelligence and education is this: intelligence will make you a good living.

JOHN MAYNARD KEYNES
1883–1946   British economist

The avoidance of taxes is the only pursuit that still carries any reward.

NIKITA KHRUSHCHEV
1894–1971   Russian statesman

Politicians are the same all over. They promise to build a bridge even where there is no river.

1960

ALEXANDER KING
1900–1965   American writer

To the majority of [newspapermen] a woman is either somebody's mother or a whore.

Rich Man, Poor Man, Freud and Fruit, 1965

That gentlemen prefer blondes is due to the fact that, apparently, pale hair, delicate skin and an infantile expression represent the very apex of a frailty which every man longs to violate.

Ibid.

FRANCIS KING
1923–   British writer

Words of delight, praise and enthusiasm are like visiting-cards. The bigger the card, the less important the man; the bigger the word, the less important the emotion.

The Listener, 1978

HUGH KINGSMILL
1889–1949   British writer and critic

A concern with the perfectibility of mankind is always a symptom of thwarted or perverted development.

RUDYARD KIPLING
1865–1936   British writer

You may carve it on his tombstone, you may cut it on his card
That a young man married is a young man marred.

'The Story of the Gadsbys', 1889

LISA KIRK
American actress

A gossip is one who talks to you about others, a bore is one who talks to you about himself; and a brilliant conversationalist is one who talks to you about yourself.

New York Journal American, 1954

ERWIN KNOLL
1931–   American editor

Everything you read in the newspapers is absoutely true, except for that rare story of which you happen to have first-hand knowledge.

RONALD KNOX
1888–1957   British writer and clergyman

It is so stupid of modern civilisation to have given up believing in the devil when he is the only explanation of it.

Let Dons Delight

ARTHUR KOESTLER
1905–1983   Hungarian-born British philosopher

Creativity in science could be described as the act of putting two and two together to make five.

The Act of Creation, 1964

The progress of science is strewn, like an ancient desert trail, with the bleached skeletons of discarded theories which once seemed to possess eternal life.

address to the PEN Club, 1976

If one looks with a cold eye at the mess man has made of his history, it is difficult to avoid the conclusion that he has been afflicted by some built-in mental disorder which drives him towards self-destruction. Murder within the species on an individual or collective scale is a phenomenon unknown in the whole animal kingdom, except for man, and a few varieties of ants and rats.

Observer, 1968

ERNIE KOVACS
1919–1962 American comedian

Television – a medium. So called because it is neither rare nor well done.

quoted in *The Filmgoer's Book of Quotes*, ed. L. Halliwell, 1973

KARL KRAUS
1874–1936 Austrian artist

A woman occasionally is quite a serviceable substitute for masturbation. It takes an abundance of imagination, to be sure.

quoted in *Die Fackel*

How is the world ruled and how do wars start? Diplomats tell lies to journalists, and they believe what they read.

Aphorisms and More Aphorisms, 1909

Journalists write because they have nothing to say, and have something to say because they write.

The devil is an optimist if he thinks he can make people meaner.

Karl Kraus by H. Zohn

Psycho-analysis is the disease of emancipated Jews; the religious ones are satisfied with diabetes.

KRIS KRISTOFFERSON
1936– American rock musician and composer

Freedom's just another word for nothing left to lose.

'Me and Bobby McGee', 1970

JOSEPH WOOD KRUTCH
1893–1970 American writer and academic

Logic is the art of going wrong with confidence.

111

STANLEY KUBRICK
1928–   American film director

The great nations have always acted like gangsters and the small nations like prostitutes.

1963

If you can talk brilliantly about a problem, it can create the consoling illusion that it has been mastered.

JEAN DE LA BRUYÈRE
1645–1696   French writer and moralist

Party loyalty lowers the greatest of men to the petty level of the masses.
Les Caractères, 1688

The shortest and best way to make your fortune is to let people see clearly that it is in their interests to promote yours.
Ibid.

A pious man is one who would be an atheist if the king were.
Ibid.

It is to receive a rare favour from a friend if, after he has achieved a high position in the world, he remembers you as an acquaintance.
Ibid.

MARQUIS DE LA GRANGE
1796–1876   French writer

When we ask advice, we are usually looking for an accomplice.
Pensées, 1872

R. D. LAING
1927–   British psychiatrist

The brotherhood of man is evoked by particular men according to their circumstances. But it seldom extends to all men. In the name of our freedom and our brotherhood we are prepared to blow up the other half of the world and to be blown up in our turn.
The Politics of Experience, 1967

Society highly values its normal men. It educates children to lose themselves and to become absurd, and thus be normal. Normal men

113

have killed perhaps 100,000,000 of their fellow normal men in the last fifty years.

Ibid.

From the moment of birth, when the Stone Age baby confronts the twentieth-century mother the baby is subjected to these forces of violence, called love, as its father and mother, and their parents and their parents before them, have been. These forces are mainly concerned with destroying most of its potential.

Ibid.

HEDY LAMARR
1913–   American film star

Any girl can be glamorous: all you have to do is stand still and look stupid.

WALTER SAVAGE LANDOR
1775–1864   British poet

Ambition is but avarice on stilts, and masked.

Despotism sits nowhere so secure as under the effigy and ensigns of Freedom.

PHILIP LARKIN
1922–   British poet

They fuck you up, your Mum and Dad.
They may not mean to, but they do.
And give you all the faults they had
And add some extra, just for you.

'This Be the Verse', 1974

FRANÇOIS, DUC DE LA ROCHEFOUCAULD
1613–1680   French aphorist

Hypocrisy is the homage that vice pays to virtue.

Maxims, 1665

Gratitude is merely a secret hope of further favours.

Ibid.

In the misfortune of our friends we find something that is not displeasing to us.

Ibid.

The love of justice in most men is nothing more than the fear of suffering injustice.

Ibid.

Old men are fond of giving good advice to console themselves for their inability to set a bad example.

Ibid.

The reason that lovers never weary each other is because they are always talking about themselves.

Ibid.

Repentance is not so much remorse for what we have done as the fear of the consequences.

Ibid.

We often do good that we may do evil with impunity.

Ibid.

We often forgive those who bore us, but we cannot forgive those whom we bore.

Ibid.

What makes other people's vanity intolerable is that it wounds our own.

Ibid.

It is easier to appear worthy of a position one does not hold, than of the office which one fills.

Ibid.

CHRISTOPHER LASCH
1932– American academic

... the classic prescription for dealing with injustice: give everybody an equal start, above all education, and meanwhile keep the niggers off your porch.

The Presidential Mystique

Nothing succeeds like the appearance of success.

The Culture of Narcissism, 1979   115

HAROLD LASKI
1893–1950   British political theorist

De mortuis nil nisi bunkum.

HELEN LAWRENSON
American journalist

Very few modern women either like or desire marriage, especially after the ceremony has been performed. Primarily women wish attention and affection. Matrimony is something they accept when there is no alternative. Really, it is a waste of time, and hazardous, to marry them. It leaves one open to a rival. Husbands, good or bad, always have rivals. Lovers, never.

Esquire magazine, 1939

STEPHEN LEACOCK
1869–1944   Canadian humorist

[A] 'Grand Old Man'. That means on our continent any one with snow white hair who has kept out of jail till eighty.

Three Score and Ten

Advertising may be described as the science of arresting the human intelligence long enough to get money from it.

PAUL LÉAUTAUD
1877–1956   French writer

The advantage of being celibate is that when one sees a pretty girl one does not need to grieve over having an ugly one back home.

Propos d'un jour, 1900

Love makes fools, marriage cuckolds, and patriotism malevolent imbeciles.

Passe-temps

ÉDOUARD LE BERQUIER
French aphorist

Visits always give pleasure: if not in the arrival, then on the departure.

Pensées des Autres

It is only the learned who care to learn, the ignorant who prefer to teach.

Ibid.

GUSTAVE LE BON
1841–1937   French aphorist

Virtuous people often revenge themselves for the constraints to which they submit by the boredom which they inspire.

Aphorismes du temps présent, 1913

FRAN LEBOWITZ
American journalist

There is no such thing as inner peace. There is only nervousness or death. Any attempt to prove otherwise constitutes unacceptable behaviour.

Metropolitan Life, 1978

The three questions of greatest concern are – 1. Is it attractive? 2. Is it amusing? 3. Does it know its place?

Ibid.

Being a woman is of special interest only to aspiring male transsexuals. To actual women it is merely a good excuse not to play football.

Ibid.

Girls who put out are tramps. Girls who don't are ladies. This is, however, a rather archaic use of the word. Should one of you boys happen upon a girl who doesn't put out, do not jump to the conclusion that you have found a lady. What you have probably found is a lesbian.

Ibid.

If you are of the opinion that the contemplation of suicide is sufficient evidence of a poetic nature, do not forget that actions speak louder than words.

Ibid.

All God's children are not beautiful. Most of God's children are, in fact, barely presentable.

Ibid.

The opposite of talking isn't listening. The opposite of talking is waiting.

Social Studies, 1981

It is imperative when flying coach that you restrain any tendency toward the vividly imaginative. For although it may momentarily appear to be the case, it is not at all likely that the cabin is entirely inhabited by crying babies smoking inexpensive domestic cigars.

Ibid.

Remember that as a teenager you are in the last stage of your life when you will be happy to hear that the phone is for you.

Ibid.

Educational television should be absolutely forbidden. It can only lead to unreasonable disappointment when your child discovers that the letters of the alphabet do not leap up out of books and dance around with royal-blue chickens.

Ibid.

Your responsibility as a parent is not as great as you might imagine. You need not supply the world with the next conqueror of disease or major motion picture star. If your child simply grows up to be someone who does not use the word 'collectible' as a noun, you can consider yourself an unqualified success.

Ibid.

Original thought is like original sin: both happened before you were born to people you could not have possibly met.

Ibid.

People (a group that in my opinion has always attracted an undue amount of attention) have often been likened to snowflakes. This analogy is meant to suggest that each is unique – no two alike. This is quite patently not the case. People . . . are quite simply a dime a dozen. And, I hasten to add, their only similarity to snowflakes resides in their invariable and lamentable tendency to turn, after a few warm days, to slush.

Ibid.

If you're going to America, bring your own food.

Ibid.

The telephone is a good way to talk to people without having to offer them a drink.

Interview magazine, 1978

STANISLAW J. LEC
1909– Polish poet and aphorist

Don't shout for help at night. You might wake your neighbours.
Unkempt Thoughts, 1962

Every stink that fights the ventilator thinks it is Don Quixote.
Ibid.

The dispensing of injustice is always in the right hands.
Ibid.

Is it progress if a cannibal uses a fork?
Ibid.

All Gods were immortal.
Ibid.

When you jump for joy, beware that no-one moves the ground from beneath your feet.
Ibid.

When smashing monuments, save the pedestals – they always come in handy.
Ibid.

GYPSY ROSE LEE
1914–1970 American striptease artiste

God is love, but get it in writing.

1975

TOM LEHRER
1928– American humorist

Life is a sewer. What you take out depends on what you put into it.

JOHN LENNON
1941–1980 British rock musician

Life is what happens to you while you're busy making other plans.
'Beautiful Boy', 1979

JOHN LENNON and PAUL McCARTNEY
1941–1980; 1942–   British rock musicians

I can make it longer if you like the style
I can change it round
and I want to be a paperback writer.

'Paperback Writer'

JOHN LEONARD
1939–   American critic

Co-opt is baby-talk for corrupt.

New York Times Book Review, 1969

The rich are different from you and me because they have more credit.

New York Times

GIACOMO, COUNT LEOPARDI
1798–1837   Italian poet and essayist

No-one is so completely disenchanted with the world, or knows it so thoroughly, or is so utterly disgusted with it, that when it begins to smile upon him he does not become partially reconciled to it.

Pensieri, 1834–7

JULIUS LESTER
1939–   American radical writer

Politics demands a certain rhetoric. It does not demand moral action to fit the rhetoric. Instead politics demands political action.

Look Out Whitey!, 1968

Black people have never rioted. A riot is what white people think blacks are involved in when they burn stores.

OSCAR LEVANT
1906–1972   American pianist and composer

Marriage is a triumph of habit over hate.

Memoirs of an Amnesiac, 1965

So little time, so little to do.

BERNARD LEVIN
1928– British journalist

What has happened to architecture since the second world war that
the only passers-by who can contemplate it without pain are those
equipped with a white stick and a dog?

The Times, 1983

Whom the mad would destroy, first they make Gods.

1967

Ask a man which way he is going to vote, and he will probably tell
you. Ask him, however, why, and vagueness is all.

Daily Mail, 1964

JOSEPH E. LEVINE
1905– American film producer

You can fool all the people all of the time if the advertising is right
and the budget is big enough.

LEONARD L. LEVINSON
1905?–1974 American anthologist

Books – what they make a movie out of for television.

SINCLAIR LEWIS
1888–1951 American novelist

... a thing called Ethics, whose nature was confusing but if you had
it you were a High-Class Realtor and if you hadn't you were a shyster,
a piker and a fly-by-night. These virtues awakened Confidence and
enabled you to handle Bigger Propositions. But they didn't imply that
you were to be impractical and refuse to take twice the value of a
house if a buyer was such an idiot that he didn't force you down on
the asking price.

Babbitt, 1922

GEORG CHRISTOPH LICHTENBERG
1742–1799   German physicist and writer

What they call 'heart' is located far lower than the fourth waistcoat button.

Aphorisms, 1764–99

Nothing is more conducive to peace of mind than not having any opinion at all.

Ibid.

He who is in love with himself has at least this advantage – he won't encounter many rivals.

Ibid.

TRYGVE LIE
1896–1968   Swedish diplomat

A real diplomat is one who can cut his neighbour's throat without having his neighbour notice it.

A. J. LIEBLING
1904–1963   American journalist

If you just try long enough and hard enough, you can always manage to boot yourself in the posterior.

The Press, 1975

ABRAHAM LINCOLN
1809–1865   American President

The Lord prefers common-looking people. That is the reason He makes so many of them.

ROBERT LINDNER
1914–1956   American psychoanalyst

Conformity, humility, acceptance – with these coins we are to pay our fares to paradise.

Must You Conform?, 1956

LIN YUTANG
1895–1976 Chinese writer

Society can only exist on the basis that there is some amount of polished lying and that no-one says exactly what he thinks.

WALTER LIPPMANN
1889–1974 American journalist

We must remember that in time of war what is said on the enemy's side of the front is always propaganda and what is said on our side of the front is truth and righteousness, the cause of humanity and a crusade for peace.

1966

Propaganda is that branch of lying which often deceives your friends without ever deceiving your enemies.
(cf. F. M. Cornford)

quoted in *The Laugh's On Me* by B. Cerf

When all think alike, then no-one is thinking.

quoted in *The Book of Laws* by H. Faber, 1980

Unless the reformer can invent something which substitutes attractive virtues for attractive vices, he will fail.

A Preface to Politics, 1914

It is perfectly true that the government is best which governs least. It is equally true that the government is best which provides most.

Ibid.

Successful democratic politicians are insecure and intimidated men. They advance politically only as they placate, appease, bribe, seduce, bamboozle or otherwise manage to manipulate the demanding and threatening elements in their constituencies.

The Public Philosophy, 1955

MARY WILSON LITTLE
fl. 1900 American writer

Men who make no pretensions to being good on one day out of seven are called sinners.

If man is only a little lower than the angels, the angels should reform.

DAVID LLOYD GEORGE
1863–1945 British Prime Minister

Doctrinaires are the vultures of principle. They feed upon principle after it is dead.

A politician is a person with whose politics you don't agree; if you agree with him he is a statesman.

1935

It is amazing how wise statesmen can be when it is ten years too late.

1932

It is easy to settle the world upon a soap box.

ARNOLD LOBEL
1933– American writer and illustrator

Nothing is harder to resist than a bit of flattery

Fables, 1980

When the need is strong there are those who will believe anything.

Ibid.

ROSS LOCKRIDGE
1914–1948 American writer

We . . . make the modern error of dignifying the Individual. We do everything we can to butter him up. We give him a name, assure him that he has certain inalienable rights, educate him, let him pass on his name to his brats and when he dies we give him a special hole in the ground . . . But after all, he's only a seed, a bloom and a withering stalk among pressing billions. Your Individual is a pretty disgusting, vain, lewd little bastard . . . By God, he has only one right guaranteed to him in Nature, and that is the right to die and stink to Heaven.

quoted in *Short Lives* by Katinka Matson, 1980

DAVID LODGE
1935– British academic and novelist

Literature is mostly about sex and not much about having children and life is the other way round.

The British Museum Is Falling Down, 1981

GEORGE LOIS
1931–   American advertising man

The business world worships mediocrity. Officially we revere free enterprise, initiative and individuality. Unofficially we fear it.
The Art of Advertising, 1977

ALICE ROOSEVELT LONGWORTH
1884–1979   American socialite

general greeting:

If you can't say anything good about someone, sit right here by me.

ANITA LOOS
1893–1981   American screenwriter

A leader of public thought in Hollywood wouldn't have sufficient mental acumen anywhere else to hold down a place in the bread line.

She always believed in the old adage – leave them while you're looking good.
Gentlemen Prefer Blondes, 1925

Kissing your hand may make you feel very good, but a diamond and sapphire bracelet lasts for ever.
Ibid.

JAMES RUSSELL LOWELL
1819–1891   American author and diplomat

Whatever you may be sure of, be sure of this: that you are dreadfully like other people.
My Study Windows, 1871

Blessed are they that have nothing to say, and who cannot be persuaded to say it.

Democracy gives every man the right to be his own oppressor.

Granting our wish is one of Fate's saddest jokes.

VICTOR LOWNES
1929–   American publisher

What is a promiscuous person – it's usually someone who is getting more sex than you are.
>> quoted in *In and Out: Debrett 1980–81* by N. Mackwood, 1980

CLARE BOOTH LUCE
1903–   American writer and diplomat

A woman's best protection is a little money of her own.
>> quoted in *The Wit of Women*

There's nothing like a good dose of another woman to make a man appreciate his wife.
>> *Ibid.*

No good deed goes unpunished.
>> quoted in *The Book of Laws* by H. Faber, 1980

EDWARD BULWER-LYTTON, LORD LYTTON
1803–1873   British author and statesman

Yield to a man's tastes and he will yield to your interests.
>> *Paul Clifford*, 1835

When you talk to the half-wise, twaddle; when you talk to the ignorant, brag; when you talk to the sagacious, look very humble and ask their opinion.
>> *Ibid.*

It is difficult to say who do you the worst mischief, enemies with the worst intentions or friends with the best.

MOMS MABLEY
American comedienne

A woman's a woman until the day she dies, but a man's only a man
as long as he can.

New York Daily News, 1975

THOMAS BABINGTON MACAULAY
1800–1859   British historian and politician

The Puritan hated bear-baiting, not because it gave pain to the bear,
but because it gave pleasure to the spectators.

We know of no spectacle so ridiculous as the British public in one of
its periodical fits of morality.

Nothing is so useless as a general maxim.

EUGENE McCARTHY
1916–   American politician

It is dangerous for a national candidate to say things that people might
remember.

Being in politics is like being a football coach. You have to be smart
enough to understand the game and dumb enough to think it's
important.

1968

MARY McCARTHY
1912–   American writer

If someone tells you he is going to make a 'realistic decision', you immediately understand that he has resolved to do something bad.

On the Contrary, 1962

It is only the middle-class people who, quite mistakenly, imagine that a lively pursuit of the latest in reading or painting will advance their status in the world.

Ibid.

DR J. D. McCOUGHEY
Australian theologian

God is dead, but fifty thousand social workers have risen to take his place.

The Bulletin magazine, 1974

GEORGE McGOVERN
1922–   American politician

The longer the title, the less important the job.

1960

NICCOLÒ MACHIAVELLI
1469–1527   Florentine political philosopher

A prince who desires to maintain his position must learn to be not always good, but to be so or not, as needs require.

The Prince, 1513

In taking possession of a state the conqueror should well reflect as to the harsh measures that may be necessary and then execute them at a single blow . . . cruelties should be committed all at once.

Ibid.

SIR ARCHIBALD McINDOE
1900–1960   British plastic surgeon

Skill is fine, and genius is splendid, but the right contacts are more valuable than either.

quoted in *The Wit of Medicine*, ed. L. and M. Cowan, 1972

WILLIAM McKINLEY
1843–1901   American President

Our differences are policies, our agreements principles.

MIGNON McLAUGHLIN
20th century American writer

We'd all like a reputation for generosity, and we'd all like to buy it cheap.
The Neurotic's Notebook, 1963

It's innocence when it charms us, ignorance when it doesn't.
Ibid.

Every society honours its live conformists and its dead troublemakers.
Ibid.

HAROLD MACMILLAN, Earl of Stockton
1894–   British Prime Minister

It has been said that there is no fool like an old fool, except a young fool. But the young fool has first to grow up to be an old fool to realise what a damn fool he was when he was a young fool.

SALVADOR DE MADARIAGA
1886–1978   Spanish writer

Considering how bad men are, it is wonderful how well they behave.
Morning Without Noon

The Anglo-Saxon conscience does not prevent the Anglo-Saxon from sinning, it merely prevents him from enjoying his sin.

MAURICE MAETERLINCK
1862–1949   Belgian essayist, poet and playwright

All our knowledge merely helps us to die a more painful death than the animals that know nothing.

The living are the dead on holiday.

RENÉ MAGRITTE
1898–1967 Belgian artist

That old question 'Who are we?' receives a disappointing answer in
the world in which we must live. Actually, we are merely the subject of
this so-called civilised world, in which intelligence, baseness, heroism
and stupidity get on very well together and are alternately being
pushed to the fore.
quoted in *Magritte: The True Art of Painting*, ed. H. Torczyner, 1979

NORMAN MAILER
1923– American writer

Women think of being a man as a gift. It is a duty. Even making love
can be a duty. A man has always got to get it up, and love isn't always
enough.

Nova magazine, 1969

Alimony is the curse of the writing classes.

1980

There are four stages to a marriage. First there's the affair, then
there's the marriage, then children and finally the fourth stage, without
which you cannot know a woman, the divorce.

Nova magazine, 1969

The horror of the Twentieth Century is the size of each event and
the paucity of its reverberation.

Of a Fire on the Moon, 1970

JOSEPH DE MAISTRE
1754–1821 French writer

Every country has the government it deserves.

letter, 1811

ANDRÉ MALRAUX
1901–1976 French writer

What is a man? A miserable little pile of secrets.

LORD MANCROFT
1914– British politician

Happy is the man with a wife to tell him what to do and a secretary to do it.

Observer, 1966

MANN'S LAW

If a scientist uncovers a publishable fact, it will become central to his theory.

Murphy's Law Book Two by A. Bloch, 1980

JAYNE MANSFIELD
1932–1967 American film star

Men are those creatures with two legs and eight hands.

HERBERT MARCUSE
1898–1979 German-born American philosopher

Not every problem someone has with his girlfriend is necessarily due to the capitalist mode of production.

The Listener, 1978

DON MARQUIS
1878–1937 American humorist

If you want to get rich from writing, write the sort of thing that's read by persons who move their lips when they're reading to themselves.

A hypocrite is a person who . . . but who isn't?
quoted in *The Oxford Book of Aphorisms*, ed. J. Gross, 1983

The more conscious a philosopher is of the weak spots of his theory, the more certain he is to speak with an air of final authority.

JUDITH MARTIN
20th century American etiquette specialist

We are all born charming, fresh and spontaneous and must be civilised before we are fit to participate in society.

Miss Manners' Guide to Excruciatingly Correct Behaviour, 1983

GROUCHO MARX
1895–1977   American comedian

No-one is completely unhappy at the failure of his best friend.

There is one way to find out if a man is honest – ask him. If he says 'Yes', you know he is crooked.

1954

KARL MARX
1818–1883   German political philosopher

Historical phenomena always happen twice – the first time as tragedy, the second as farce.

THOMAS MASARYCK
Czech politician

Dictators always look good until the last minutes.

MATZ'S MAXIM

A conclusion is the place where you got tired of thinking.

quoted in *Murphys's Law Book Two* by A. Bloch, 1980

W. SOMERSET MAUGHAM
1874–1965   British novelist and playwright

A man marries to have a home, but also because he doesn't want to be bothered with sex and all that sort of thing.

The Circle, 1921

When from time to time I have seen the persons with whom the great lovers satisfied their desires, I have often been more astonished by the robustness of their appetites than envious of their successes. It is obvious that you need not often go hungry if you are willing to dine off mutton hash and turnip tops.

The Summing Up, 1938

Love is only a dirty trick played on us to achieve the continuation of the species.

A Writer's Notebook, 1949

Constance: I'm tired of being the modern wife.
Martha: What do you mean by the modern wife?
Constance: A prostitute who doesn't deliver the goods.

The Constant Wife

A woman will always sacrifice herself if you give her the opportunity. It is her favourite form of self-indulgence.

You can't learn too soon that the most useful thing about a principle is that it can always be sacrificed to expediency.

The Circle, 1921

Hypocrisy is the most difficult and nerve-racking vice that any man can pursue; it needs an unceasing vigilance and a rare detachment of spirit. It cannot, like adultery or gluttony, be practised at spare moments; it is a wholetime job.

Cakes and Ale, 1930

From the earliest times the old have rubbed it into the young that they are wiser than they, and before the young had discovered what nonsense this was they were old too, and it profited them to carry on the imposture.

Ibid.

I'll give you my opinion of the human race in a nutshell . . . their heart's in the right place, but their head is a thoroughly inefficient organ.

The Summing Up, 1938

Most people have a furious itch to talk about themselves and are restrained only by the disinclination of others to listen. Reserve is an artificial quality that is developed in most of us as the result of inumerable rebuffs.

Ibid.

I forget who it was that recommended men for their soul's good to do each day two things they disliked . . . it is a precept that I have

133

followed scrupulously; for every day I have got up and I have gone to bed.

The Moon and Sixpence, 1919

I don't think you want too much sincerity in society. It would be like an iron girder in a house of cards.

The Circle, 1921

Love is what happens to a man and women who don't know each other.

Dying is a very dull, dreary affair. My advice to you is to have nothing whatever to do with it.

last words, 1956

BILL MAULDIN
1921–   American cartoonist

'Peace' is when nobody's shooting. A 'just peace' is when our side gets what it wants.

quoted in *Loose Talk*, ed. L. Botts, 1980

FRANÇOIS MAURIAC
1885–1970   French novelist and playwright

Human love is often but the encounter of two weaknesses.

Cain, Where Is Your Brother?, 1962

ANDRE MAUROIS (Émile Herzog)
1885–1967   French writer

The only thing experience teaches us is that experience teaches us nothing.

LOUIS B. MAYER
1885–1957   American film magnate

Look out for yourself – or they'll pee on your grave.

MARGARET MEAD
1901–1978   American anthropologist

Women want mediocre men, and men are working hard to become as mediocre as possible.

Quote magazine, 1958

H. L. MENCKEN
1880–1956   American editor, essayist and philologist

The urge to save humanity is almost always a false front for the urge to rule.

Minority Report, 1956

Politics, as hopeful men practise it in the world, consists mainly of the delusion that a change in form is a change in substance.

Prejudices, 4th series, 1924

Voting is simply a way of determining which side is the stronger without putting it to the test of fighting.

Minority Report, 1956

When I hear a man applauded by the mob I always feel a pang of pity for him. All he has to do to be hissed is to live long enough.

Ibid.

The chief business of the nation, as a nation, is the setting up of heroes, mostly bogus.

Prejudices, 3rd series, 1922

A good politician is quite as unthinkable as an honest burglar.

Minority Report, 1956

... democracy is grounded upon so childish a complex of fallacies that they must be protected by a rigid system of taboos, else even halfwits would argue it to pieces. Its first concern must thus be to penalise the free play of ideas.

In Defense of Women, 1923

A sense of humour always withers in the presence of the messianic delusion, like justice and truth in front of patriotic passion.

Prejudices

The demagogue is one who preaches doctrines he knows to be untrue to men he knows to be idiots.

I know of no existing nation that deserves to live. And I know of very few individuals.

Democracy is a form of religion. It is the worship of jackals by jackasses.

Sententiae, 1916

Under democracy, one party always devotes its chief energies to trying to prove that the other party is unfit to rule – and both commonly succeed, and are right.

Minority Report, 1956

Democracy is the theory that the common people know what they want, and deserve to get it good and hard.

A Book of Burlesques, 1920

The most popular man under a democracy is not the most democratic man, but the most despotic man. The common folk delight in the exactions of such a man. They like him to boss them. Their natural gait is the goosestep.

What men value in this world is not rights, but privileges.

Minority Report, 1956

Metaphysics is almost always an attempt to prove the incredible by an appeal to the unintelligible.

Ibid.

There are no dull subjects. There are only dull writers.

quoted in *Esquire* magazine, 1965

To die for an idea – it is unquestionably noble. But how much nobler it would be if men died for ideas that were true.

Conscience is the inner voice that warns us that someone might be looking.

A Mencken Chrestomathy, 1949

We must respect the other fellow's religion, but only in the sense and to the extent that we respect his theory that his wife is beautiful and his children smart.

Minority Report, 1956

God is the immemorial refuge of the incompetent, the helpless, the miserable. They find not only sanctuary in His arms, but also a kind of superiority, soothing to their macerated egos; He will set them above their betters.

Ibid.

It takes a long while for a naturally trustful person to reconcile himself to the idea that after all God will not help him.

Ibid.

Of learned men, the clergy show the lowest development of professional ethics. Any pastor is free to cadge customers from the divines of rival sects, and to denounce the divines themselves as theological quacks.

Ibid.

Puritanism – the haunting fear that someone, somewhere, may be happy.

A Book of Burlesques, 1920

A man's women folk, whatever their outward show of respect for his merit and authority, always regard him secretly as an ass, and with something akin to pity . . . In this fact, perhaps, lies one of the best proofs of feminine intelligence or, as the common phrase makes it, feminine intuition.

In Defense of Women, 1923

Alimony – the ransom that the happy pay to the devil.

A Book of Burlesques, 1920

When women kiss it always remind one of prize fighters shaking hands.

Sententiae, 1916

The allurement that women hold out to men is precisely the allurement that Cape Hatteras holds out to sailors: they are enormously dangerous and hence enormously fascinating.

The Smart Set magazine, 1919

Q: If you find so much that is unworthy of reverence in the United States, why do you live here?
Mencken: Why do men go to zoos?

Prejudices, 5th series, 1926

Is it hot in the rolling mill? Are the hours long? Is $15 a day not enough? Then escape is very easy. Simply throw up your job, spit on your hands, and write another 'Rosenkavalier'.

Sententiae, 1916

Psychotherapy – the theory that the patient will probably get well anyhow, and is certainly a damned ijjit.

Ibid

Lawyer – one who protects us against robbers by taking away the temptation.

Ibid

Husbands never become good. They merely become proficient.

Ibid

Before a man speaks it is always safe to assume that he is a fool. After he speaks, it is seldom necessary to assume it.

Ibid

Popularity – the capacity for listening sympathetically when men boast of their wives and women complain of their husbands.

Ibid

Truth – something somehow discreditable to someone.

Ibid

Self-respect – the secure feeling that no-one, as yet, is suspicious.

Ibid

Remorse – regret that one waited so long to do it.

Ibid

The difference between a moral man and a man of honour is that the latter regrets a discreditable act, even when it has worked and he has not been caught.

Ibid

An idealist is one who, on noticing that a rose smells better than a cabbage, concludes that it will also make better soup.

Ibid

Men are the only animals that devote themselves, day in and day out, to making one another unhappy. It is an art like any other. Its virtuosi are called altruists.

Ibid

Evil is that which one believes of others. It is a sin to believe evil of others, but it is seldom a mistake.

Ibid

Whenever you hear a man speak of his love for his country, it is a sign that he expects to be paid for it.

Ibid.

Friendship is a common belief in the same fallacies, mountebanks and hobgoblins.

Ibid.

When a man laughs at his troubles he loses a great many friends. They never forgive the loss of their prerogative.

Ibid.

Say what you like about the Ten Commandments, you must always come back to the pleasant fact that there are only ten of them.

Ibid.

GEORGE MIKES
1912–   Czech humorist

Continental people have a sex life; the English have hot-water bottles.
How to Be an Alien, 1946

ARTHUR MILLER
1915–   American playwright

I have always felt that concentration camps . . . are the logical conclusion of contemporary life.
Writers at Work, 3rd series, 1967

HENRY MILLER
1891–1980   American writer

The democratic disease which expresses its tyranny by reducing everything to the level of the herd.

The Wisdom of the Heart, 1941

JONATHAN MILLER
1936–   British doctor, writer and director

Holidays are an expensive trial of strength. The only satisfaction comes from survival.
Daily Herald, 1962

MAX MILLER
1895–1963   British comedian

There was a little girl
Who had a little curl
Right in the middle of her forehead.
When she was good, she was very, very good
And when she was bad, she was very, very popular.

The Max Miller Blue Book

KATE MILLETT
1934–   American feminist

Aren't women prudes if they don't and prostitutes if they do?

speech, 1975

SPIKE MILLIGAN
1918–   British comedian

Render any politician down and there's enough fat to fry an egg.

1968

MINISTRY OF INFORMATION

What is truth? We must adopt a pragmatic definition: it is what is
believed to be the truth. A lie that is put across therefore becomes
the truth and may, therefore, be justified. The difficulty is to keep up
lying . . . it is simpler to tell the truth and if a sufficient emergency
arises, to tell one, big thumping lie that will then be believed.

memo on the maintenance of British civilian morale, 1939

NANCY MITFORD
1904–1973   British writer

I love children. Especially when they cry – for then someone takes
them away.

ADDISON MIZNER and OLIVER HERFORD
1872–1933; 1863–1935   American architect; American writer

Actresses will happen in the best regulated families.

The Entirely New Cynic's Calendar, 1905

WILSON MIZNER
1876–1933 American gambler, sportsman and wit

If you steal from one author it's plagiarism; if you steal from many it's research.

Some of the greatest love affairs I've known have involved one actor, unassisted.
> quoted in *The Incredible Mizners* by A. Johnson, 1953

I respect faith, but doubt is what gives you an education.
> quoted in *H. L. Mencken's Dictionary of Quotations*, 1942

Be nice to people on the way up, because you'll meet them on your way down.
> quoted in *The Incredible Mizners* by A. Johnson, 1953

A drama critic is a person who surprises a playwright by informing him what he meant.
> quoted in *The People's Almanac*, 1976

Insanity is considered a ground for divorce, though by the very same token it is the shortest detour to marriage.
> *Ibid.*

I've spent several years in Hollywood, and I still think the movie heroes are in the audience.

WALTER MONDALE
1928– American politician

If you are sure you understand everything that is going on, you are hopelessly confused.
> 1978

ASHLEY MONTAGU
1905– British writer

Love, for too many people in our time, consists of sleeping with a seductive woman, one who is properly endowed with the right distribution of curves and conveniences, and one upon whom a permanent lien has been acquired through the institution of marriage.
> *The Natural Superiority of Women*

C. E. MONTAGUE
1867–1928   British writer

War hath no fury like a non-combatant.

Disenchantment, 1922

MICHEL DE MONTAIGNE
1533–1592   French moralist and essayist

Nothing is so firmly believed as that which we least know.

A good marriage would be between a blind wife and a deaf husband.

Is there anything so assured, resolved, disdainful, contemplative, solemn and serious as an ass?

CHARLES, BARON DE MONTESQUIEU
1689–1755   French philosopher, writer and lawyer

An author is a fool who, not content with having bored those who have lived with him, insists on boring future generations.

Liberty is the right to do what the laws permit.

De l'esprit des lois, 1748

Mediocrity is a hand-rail.

Mes pensées, 1722–55

HENRY DE MONTHERLANT
1896–1973   French writer

Beauty is still supposed to arouse desire. This is not the case. Beauty has nothing to do with the physical jerks underneath the coverlet. Ugliness is one of the most reliable stimulants.

The Goddess Cypris, 1944

Most affections are habits or duties we lack the courage to end.

Queen after Death, 1942

GEORGE MOORE
1852–1933   Irish writer

There is always a right and a wrong way, and the wrong way always
seems the more reasonable.

ALBERTO MORAVIA
1907– Italian writer

The ratio of literacy to illiteracy is constant, but nowadays the illiterates can read.

Observer, 1979

ROBIN MORGAN
1941– American feminist

Don't accept rides from strange men – and remember that all men are as strange as hell.

Sisterhood Is Powerful, 1970

Woman is: finally screwing and your groin and buttocks and thighs ache like hell and you're all wet and maybe bloody and it wasn't like a Hollywood movie at all but Jesus at least you're not a virgin any more but is this what it's all about? And meanwhile, he's asking 'Did you come?'

Ibid.

CHRISTOPHER MORLEY
1890–1957 American novelist and essayist

Only the sinner has the right to preach.

JOHN, VISCOUNT MORLEY
1838–1923 British statesman and writer

Where it is a duty to worship the sun it is pretty sure to be a crime to examine the laws of heat.

Voltaire, 1872

RAYMOND MORTIMER
1895–1980 British literary critic

Tact is the art of convincing people that they know more than you do.

Conversation is anecdote tempered by interruption.

BILL MOYERS
American government official

There are honest journalists like there are honest politicians. When bought they stay bought.

MALCOLM MUGGERIDGE
1903– British journalist

Never . . . was any generation of men intent upon the pursuit of happiness more advantageously placed to attain it who yet, with seeming deliberation, took the opposite course – towards chaos, not order, towards breakdown, not stability, towards death, destruction and darkness, not life, creativity and light.

Esquire magazine, 1970

There is no snobbishness like that of professional equalitarians.

Chronicles of Wasted Time, vol. I, 1978

Human life . . . is only theatre, and mostly cheap melodrama at that.

Tread Softly for You Tread on My Jokes, 1966

A ready means of being cherished by the English is to adopt the simple expedient of living a long time.

Esquire magazine, 1961

ANKA MUHLSTEIN
French writer

The parvenu is always someone else.

The Rise of the French Rothschilds, 1983

MURPHY'S LAW OF RESEARCH

Enough research will tend to support your theory.

quoted in *Murphy's Law* by A. Bloch, 1979

ALFRED DE MUSSET
1810–1857 French poet and playwright

The most disagreeable thing that your worst enemy says to your face does not approach what your best friends say behind your back.

quoted in *A Cynic's Breviary* by J. R. Solly, 1925

NAPOLEON BONAPARTE
1769–1821   Emperor of France

A man will fight harder for his interests than for his rights.

Maxims, 1804–15

One never climbs so high as when he knows not where he is going.

Ibid.

Put a rogue in the limelight and he will act like an honest man.

Ibid.

History is the version of past events that people have decided to agree on.

Ibid.

The greatest general is he who makes the fewest mistakes.

Ibid.

GEORGE JEAN NATHAN
1882–1958   American critic

Politics is the diversion of trivial men who, when they succeed at it, become important in the eyes of more trivial men.

1954

What passes for woman's intuition is often nothing more than man's transparency.

Bad officials are elected by good citizens who do not vote.

I know many married men, I even know a few happily married men, but I don't know one who wouldn't fall down the first open coal-hole running after the first pretty girl who gave him a wink.

quoted in *Men Against Women*, ed. C. Neider   145

Patriotism is often an arbitrary veneration of real estate above principles.

JAWAHARLAL NEHRU
1889–1964 Indian Prime Minister

You don't change the course of history by turning the faces of portraits to the wall.

HAROLD NICOLSON
1886–1968 British politician and writer

We are all inclined to judge ourselves by our ideals; others by their acts.

FRIEDRICH WILHELM NIETZSCHE
1844–1900 German philosopher

He who despises himself nevertheless esteems himself as a self-despiser.

One never dives into the water to save a drowning man more eagerly than when there are others present who dare not take the risk.

The soul must have its chosen sewers to carry away its ordure. This function is performed by persons, relationships, professions, the fatherland, the world, or finally, for the really arrogant – I mean our modern pessimists – by the Good God himself.

'Every man has his price'. This is not true. But for every man there exists a bait which he cannot resist swallowing.

A politician divides mankind into two classes; tools and enemies. That means he knows only one class – enemies.

Liberal institutions straightway cease from being liberal the moment they are soundly established: once this is attained, no more grievous and more thorough enemies of freedom exist than liberal institutions.

1888

Love matches, so called, have illusion for their father and need for their mother.

The preponderance of pain over pleasure is the cause of our fictitious morality and religion.

We praise or blame according to whether the one or the other offers
a greater opportunity for our power of judgment to shine out.
Human, All Too Human, 1878

There are men who desire power simply for the sake of the happiness
it will bring; these belong chiefly to political parties.
The Will to Power, 1888

A casual stroll through a lunatic asylum shows that faith does not
prove anything.

Which is it: is man one of God's blunders, or is God one of man's
blunders?

'I have done that', says my memory. 'I cannot have done that', says
my pride, and remains silent. At last – memory yields.
Beyond Good and Evil, 1886

'NIGHT AFTER NIGHT'

Anon.: Goodness, what beautiful diamonds!
Mae West: Goodness had nothing to do with it, dearie.
screenplay Vincent Lawrence and Mae West, 1932

RICHARD M. NIXON
1913–   American President

Lansdale seized on the idea of using Nixon to build support for the
[Vietnamese] elections . . . really honest elections, this time. 'Oh, sure,
honest, yes, that's right,' Nixon said, 'so long as you win!' With that
he winked, drove his elbow into Lansdale's arm and slapped his own
knee.
quoted in *Sideshow* by W. Shawcross, 1979

You know very well that whether you are on page one or page thirty
depends on whether [the press] fear you. It is just as simple as that.

No television performance takes as much preparation as an off-the-
cuff talk.

CHARLES NODIER
1780–1844   French writer

Our years, our debts, and our enemies are always more numerous than we imagine.

BARRY NORMAN
1933–   British critic

Perhaps at fourteen every boy should be in love with some ideal woman to put on a pedestal and worship. As he grows up, of course, he will put her on a pedestal the better to view her legs.

quoted in The Listener, 1978

WILLIAM C. O'BRIEN
British radical

Violence is the way of ensuring a hearing for moderation.

quoted in the Observer, 1981

F. S. OLIVER
1864–1934   British writer

A wise politician will never grudge a genuflexion or a rapture if it is expected of him by the prevalent opinion.

AUSTIN O'MALLEY
1858–1932   American oculist and writer

God shows his contempt for wealth by the kind of person he selects to receive it.

It is a mean thief, or a successful author that plunders the dead.

Show me a genuine case of platonic friendship and I shall show you two old or homely faces.

BRIAN O'NOLAN (Myles na Gopaleen, Flann O'Brien)
1910–1966   Irish writer

What is important is food, money and opportunities for scoring off one's enemies. Give a man these three things and you won't hear much squawking out of him.

The Best of Myles, 1968

MARCEL OPHULS
French film director

Puritanism . . . helps us enjoy our misery while we are inflicting it on others.

The Listener, 1978

J. ROBERT OPPENHEIMER
1904–1967   American nuclear physicist

The optimist thinks that this is the best of all possible worlds, and the pessimist knows it.

Bulletin of the Atomic Scientists, 1951

JOSÉ ORTEGA Y GASSET
1883–1955   Spanish philosopher and statesman

Civilisation is nothing else but the attempt to reduce force to being the last resort.

A revolution only lasts fifteen years – a period which coincides with the effectiveness of a generation.

1930

An idea is putting truth in checkmate.

The Revolt of the Masses, 1930

JOE ORTON
1933–1967   British playwright

Fay: The British police force used to be run by men of integrity.
Truscott: That is a mistake which has been rectified.

Loot, 1966

Kath: Can he be present at the birth of his child?
Ed: It's all any reasonable child can expect if the dad is present at the conception.

Entertaining Mr. Sloane, 1964

GEORGE ORWELL (Eric Blair)
1903–1950   British novelist and essayist

History is full of ignominious getaways by the great and famous.

Who Are the War Criminals, 1942

Liberal – a power worshipper without power.

In our time, political speech and writing are largely the defence of the indefensible.

> *Politics and the English Language*, 1950

Political language . . . is designed to make lies sound truthful and murder respectable and to give an appearance of solidarity to pure wind.

> *Ibid.*

Serious sport has nothing to do with fair play. It is bound up with hatred, jealousy, boastfulness, disregard of all rules and sadistic pleasure in witnessing violence: in other words it is war minus the shooting.

> *The Sporting Spirit*, 1945

Most people get a fair amount of fun out of their lives, but on balance life is suffering and only the very young or the very foolish imagine otherwise.

> *Shooting an Elephant*, 1950

One wants to stay alive, of course, but one only stays alive by virtue of the fear of death.

> *Ibid.*

For the ordinary man is passive. Within a narrow circle . . . he feels himself master of his fate, but against major events he is as helpless as against the elements. So far from endeavouring to influence the future, he simply lies down and lets things happen to him.

Advertising is the rattling of a stick inside a swill bucket.

Saints should always be judged guilty until they are proved innocent.

> *Reflections on Gandhi*, 1949

OVID (P. Ovidius Naso)
?43 BC – AD 17   Roman poet

Whether a pretty woman grants or withholds her favours, she always likes to be asked for them.

> *Ars Amatoria, c.* AD 8

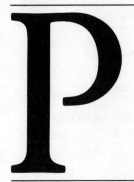

MARCEL PAGNOL
1894–1974 French playwright

One has to look out for engineers – they begin with sewing machines and end up with the atomic bomb.

Critique des critiques, 1949

The most difficult secret for a man to keep is his own opinion of himself.

1954

THOMAS PAINE
1737–1809 British radical

Society is produced by our wants and government by our wickedness.

Common Sense, 1776

DOROTHY PARKER
1893–1967 American poet and screenwriter

The only 'ism' Hollywood believes in is plagiarism.

By the time you swear you're his
shivering and sighing
and he vows his passion is
infinite, undying –
Lady, make a note of this:
One of you is lying.

'Unfortunate Coincidence', 1927

The two most beautiful words in the English language are 'Cheque Enclosed'.

Drink and dance and laugh and lie
Love, the reeling midnight through
For tomorrow we shall die!
(But, alas, we never do.)

           'The Flaw in Paganism', 1931

Lady, lady, should you meet
One whose ways are all discreet,
One who murmurs that his wife
Is the lodestar of his life,
One who keeps assuring you
That he never was untrue,
Never loved another one . . .
Lady, lady, better run!

           'Social Note', 1927

The sweeter the apple, the blacker the core –
Scratch a lover and find a foe!

      'Ballade of a Great Weariness', 1927

My soul is crushed, my spirit sore
I do not like me anymore,
I cavil, quarrel, grumble, grouse
I ponder on the narrow house
I shudder at the thought of men
I'm due to fall in love again.

        from *Enough Rope*, 1927

The man she had was kind and clean
And well enough for every day,
But oh, dear friends, you should have seen
The one that got away.

        'The Fisherwoman', 1931

Where's the man could ease a heart
Like a satin gown?

        'The Satin Dress', 1927

A girl's best friend is her mutter.

      quoted in *Wits End*, ed. R. Drennan, 1968

Life is a glorious cycle of song,
A medley of extemporania;
And love is a thing that can never go wrong;
And I am Marie of Roumania.

        'Comment', 1927   153

Every love's the love before
In a duller dress.

'Summary', 1931

Everything's great in this good old world;
(This is the stuff they can always use.)
God's in his heaven, the hill's dew-pearled;
(This will provide for baby's shoes.)
Hunger and War do not mean a thing;
Everything's rosy where'er we roam;
Hark, how the little birds gaily sing!
(This is what fetches the bacon home.)

'The Far Sighted Muse', c. 1925

Razors pain you;
Rivers are damp;
Acids stain you;
And drugs cause cramp.
Guns aren't lawful;
Nooses give;
Gas smells awful;
You might as well live.

'Résumé', 1927

ROBERT B. PARKER
1932–   American writer

Fourteen years in the professor dodge has taught me that one can argue
ingeniously on behalf of any theory, applied to any piece of literature.
This is rarely harmful, because normally no-one reads such essays.

quoted in *Murder Ink*, ed. D. Wynn, 1977

SIDNEY PATERNOSTER

Love may laugh at locksmiths, but he has a profound respect for money
bags.

The Folly of the Wise, 1907

CESARE PAVESE
1908–1950   Italian novelist

Many men on the point of an edifying death would be furious if they

were suddenly restored to health.
> quoted in *The Faber Book of Aphorisms*,
> ed. Auden and Kronenberger, 1964

No woman marries for money: they are all clever enough, before marrying a millionaire, to fall in love with him first.
> *The Business of Living: Diaries 1935–50*

The art of living is the art of knowing how to believe lies.
> *The Burning Brand*, 1961

Mistakes are always initial.
> quoted in *The Faber Book of Aphorisms*,
> ed. Auden and Kronenberger, 1964

KEITH J. PENDRED
British scientist

Successful research impedes further successful research.
> *Bulletin of the Atomic Scientists*, 1963

WILLIAM PENN
1644–1718   Founder of Pennsylvania

Let the people think they govern and they will be governed.
> 1693

BOIES PENROSE
b. 1902   American politician

Public office is the last refuge of a scoundrel.
> 1931

LAURENCE J. PETER
1919–   Canadian educator

Democracy is a process by which the people are free to choose the man who will get the blame.
> *Peter's Quotations*, 1977

A bore is a fellow talking who can change the subject back to his topic of conversation faster than you can change it back to yours.

Ibid.

Education is a method whereby one acquires a higher grade of prejudices.

Ibid.

Psychiatry enables us to correct our faults by confessing our parents' shortcomings.

Peter's Principles, 1977

In a hierarchy every employee tends to rise to his level of incompetence ... in time every post tends to be occupied by an employee who is incompetent to carry out its duties ... Work is accomplished by those employees who have not yet reached their level of incompetence.

The Peter Principle, 1969

HENRI PETIT
1900– French writer

One despairs of others so as not to despair too much of oneself.

Les Justes Solitudes

WILLIAM LYON PHELPS
1865–1943 American businessman

Nature makes boys and girls lovely to look upon so they can be tolerated until they acquire some sense.

SIR ARTHUR WING PINERO
1855–1934 British dramatist

How many 'coming men' has one known! Where on earth do they all go to?

WILLIAM PITT, the Younger
1759–1806 British Prime Minister

Necessity is the plea for every infringement of human freedom. It is the argument of tyrants; it is the creed of slaves.

1783

PLATO
428–347 BC   Greek philosopher

The punishment which the wise suffer, who refuse to take part in the government, is, to live under the government of worse men.

DONN PLATT

There is no tyranny so despotic as that of public opinion among a free people.

WILLIS PLAYER
1915–   American writer

A liberal is a person whose interests aren't at stake at the moment.

San Diego Tribune

KONSTANTIN POBEDONOSTSEV
1827–1907   Russian jurist

Parliaments are the great lie of our time.

1896

CHANNING POLLOCK
1880–1946   American dramatist

A critic is a legless man who teaches running.

GEORGES POMPIDOU
1911–1974   French President

A statesman is a politician who places himself at the service of the nation. A politician is a statesman who places the nation at his service.

Observer, 1873

FRANCIS PONGE
1899–   French writer

History – that little sewer where man loves to wallow.

ALEXANDER POPE
1688–1744   British poet

Amusement is the happiness of those who cannot think.

O Death, all-eloquent! you only prove
What dust we dote on, when 'tis man we love.
                                    'Eloisa to Abelard', 1717

Party is the madness of the many for the gain of the few.
(cf. Swift)

ANTONIO PORCHIA
b. 1886   Argentine writer

If you do not raise your eyes, you will think that you are the highest
point.
                                                    Voces, 1943

ADAM CLAYTON POWELL, Jr.
1908–1972   American politician

Beware of Greeks bearing gifts, coloured men looking for loans, and
whites who understand the negro.

J. ENOCH POWELL
1912–   British politician

History is littered with wars which everybody knew would never
happen.
                                                        1967

AUGUSTE PRÉAULT
1809–1879   French writer

What the crowd requires is mediocrity of the highest order.

DON K. PRICE
1910–   American academic

It's easier to be a liberal a long way from home.

V. S. PRITCHETT
1900–   British novelist, short-story writer and critic

The principle of procrastinated rape is said to be the ruling one in all the great best-sellers.

The Living Novel and Other Appreciations, 1964

'PRIVATE EYE' magazine

History repeats itself – the first time as tragi-comedy, the second time as bedroom farce.

1978

'PRIVATE WORLDS'

Samuel Hinds: We hate the people we love because they're the only ones that can hurt us.

screenplay by Lyn Starling, 1935

'THE PRODUCERS'

Zero Mostel: That's it baby! When you got it, flaunt it! Flaunt it!

screenplay by Mel Brooks, 1968

PIERRE-JOSEPH PROUDHON
1809–1865   French radical writer

To be governed is to be watched, inspected, spied upon, directed, law-ridden, regulated, penned up, indoctrinated, preached at, checked, appraised, seized, censured, commanded by beings who have neither title, knowledge nor virtue.

MARCEL PROUST
1871–1922   French novelist

The fact of a man's having proclaimed (as leader of a political party, or in any other capacity) that it is wicked to lie obliges him as a rule to lie more than other people.

Remembrance of Things Past, 1913–27

The fixity of a habit is generally in direct proportion to its absurdity.

Ibid.   159

DAVID PRYCE-JONES
1936– British writer

When you're bored with yourself, marry, and be bored with someone else.

Owls and Satyrs

PUBLIUS SYRUS
fl. 1st century BC Roman philosopher

If you would live innocently, seek solitude.

Moral Sayings

A cock has great influence on his own dunghill.

Ibid.

RAYMOND QUENEAU
1903–1976   French historian

History is the study of man's unhappiness.

A Model History

L. A. J. QUÉTELET
1796–1874   Belgian statistician

Society . . . prepares crimes; criminals are only the instruments necessary for executing them.

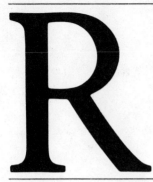

FRANÇOIS RABELAIS
1495?–1533   French physician, scholar and writer

I owe much; I have nothing; the rest I leave to the poor.

last words, 1533

If you wish to avoid seeing a fool you must first break your mirror.

MILTON RAKOVE
1918–   American academic

A citizen is influenced by principle in direct proportion to his distance from the political situation.

Virginia Quarterly Review, 1965

TONY RANDALL
1920–   American film actor

Compassion is a luxury of the affluent.

quoted in *Playboy* magazine, 1974

SAM RAYBURN
1882–1961   American politician

maxim:

If you want to get along, go along.

CHARLES READE
1814–1884   British novelist

We go on fancying that each man is thinking of us, but he is not; he is like us: he is thinking of himself.

RONALD REAGAN
1911–   American film star and President

Government is like a baby. An alimentary canal with a big appetite at one end and no sense of responsibility at the other.

Saturday Evening Post, 1965

REX REED
1938–   American journalist

In Hollywood, if you don't have happiness, you send out for it.

THOMAS B. REED
1839–1902

A statesman is a successful politician who is dead.

HENRI DE RÉGNIER
1864–1936   French poet and novelist

It is well to write love letters. There are certain things it is not easy to ask your mistress for face to face, like money, for instance.

CHARLES DE RÉMUSAT
1797–1875   French writer

Unanimity is almost an indication of servitude.

JULES RENARD
1864–1910   French novelist and playwright

Look for the ridiculous in everything and you find it.

Journal, 1890

Do not ask me to be kind; just ask me to act as though I were.

Ibid., 1898

JAMES RESTON
1909– American journalist

All politics are based on the indifference of the majority.

1968

A government is the only known vessel that leaks from the top.

This is the devilish thing about foreign affairs: they are foreign and will not always conform to our whim.

1964

PIERRE REVERDY
1889–1960 French writer

One is vain by nature, modest by necessity.

En vrac

One lives with so many bad deeds on one's conscience and some good intentions in one's heart.

Le Livre de mon bord

ROBERT RICE
1916– American writer

Crime is a logical extension of the sort of behaviour that is often considered perfectly respectable in legitimate business.

The Business of Crime, 1956

SIR RALPH RICHARDSON
1902–1983 British actor

The art of acting consists in keeping people from coughing.

Observer, 1947

CARDINAL RICHELIEU
1585–1642 French statesman and prelate

Secrecy is the first essential in affairs of state.

Testament politique, 1641

DAVID RIESMAN
1909–   American sociologist

The media, far from being a conspiracy to dull the political sense of the people, could be viewed as a conspiracy to disguise the extent of political indifference.

ANTOINE RIVAROLI, COMTE DE RIVAROL
1753–1801   French journalist

There are some men who gain from their wealth only the fear of losing it.

L'Esprit de Rivarol, 1808

JOHN P. ROCHE
1923–   American journalist

In politics, a straight line is the shortest distance to disaster.

Albany Times-Union, 1976

SAMUEL ROGERS
1763–1855   British poet

It doesn't much signify whom one marries, for one is sure to find out the next morning that it was someone else.

Table Talk

WILL ROGERS
1879–1935   American humorist

You can't say civilisation don't advance . . . for in every war they kill you a new way.

The Autobiography of Will Rogers, 1949

Liberty don't work as good in practice as it does in Speech.

1927

Democracy is the art of saying 'nice doggie' until you can find a rock.

ERNST RÖHM
1887–1934   German Nazi leader

Brutality is respected. The people need wholesome fear. They want to
fear something. They want someone to frighten them and make them
shudderingly submissive . . . Why babble about brutality and get
indignant about tortures. The masses want them. They need
something that will give them a thrill of horror.

MIKE ROMANOFF
1890–1972   American restaurateur

Work is the curse of the drinking classes.

KARYL ROOSEVELT

Drunks are rarely amusing unless they know some good songs and lose
a lot at poker.

New York Times, 1975

JEAN ROSTAND
b. 1894   French scientist and writer

Kill one man and you are a murderer. Kill millions and you are a
conqueror. Kill all and you are a God.

Thoughts of a Biologist, 1955

Literature: proclaiming in front of everyone what one is careful to
conceal from one's immediate circle.

Journal d'un caractère, 1931

Never feel remorse for what you have thought about your wife. She
has thought much worse things about you.

Le Mariage, 1927

God, that dumping ground of our dreams.

A Biologist's Notebook

LEO ROSTEN
1908–   American writer

Most men do not mature, they simply grow taller.

Saturday Review, 1970

PHILIP ROTH
1933–   American novelist

The Jewish man with parents alive is a fifteen-year-old boy and will remain a fifteen-year-old boy until they die.

Portnoy's Complaint, 1969

JEAN-JACQUES ROUSSEAU
1712–1778   French philosopher

The first man to fence in a piece of land saying 'This is mine' and who found people simple enough to believe him, was the real founder of civil society.

Discourse on the Origin and Bases of Inequality among Men, 1754

The English people fancy they are free; it is only during the election of Members of Parliament that they are so. As soon as these are elected the people are slaves . . . In the brief moments of their liberation the abuse made of it fully deserves that it should be lost.

CARL ROWAN
1925–   American diplomat

There aren't any embarrassing questions – only embarrassing answers.

New Yorker magazine, 1963

HELEN ROWLAND
1875–1950   American writer

A bachelor never quite gets over the idea that he is a thing of beauty and a boy for ever.

A bachelor has to have inspiration for making love to a woman, a married man needs only an excuse.

R

Every man wants a woman to appeal to his better side, his nobler instincts and his higher nature – and another woman to help him forget them.

A Guide to Men

The follies which a man regrets most in his life are those which he didn't commit when he had the opportunity.

The hardest task in a girl's life is to prove to a man that his intentions are serious.

Reflections of a Bachelor Girl, 1903

A husband is what's left of the lover once the nerve has been extracted.

In olden times sacrifices were made at the altar – a practice which is still continued.

Love, the quest; marriage, the conquest; divorce, the inquest.

It isn't tying himself to one woman that a man dreads when he thinks of marrying; it's separating himself from all the others.

Marriage – a souvenir of love.

One man's folly is another man's wife.

When you see what some girls marry, you realise how much they must hate to work for a living.

Woman: the peg on which the wit hangs his jest, the preacher his text, the cynic his grouch and the sinner his justification.

There is a vast difference between the savage and civilised man, but it is never apparent to their wives until after breakfast.

A Guide to Men

'RUDE PRAVO'

Those who lie on the rails of history must expect to have their legs chopped off.

Czech party newspaper, quoted in *The Listener*, 1979

S. A. RUDIN
Canadian psychologist

In a crisis that forces a choice to be made among alternative courses
of action, most people will choose the worst one possible.

New Republic, 1961

DAMON RUNYON
1884–1946   American journalist and writer

The race is not always to the swift, nor the battle to the strong, but
that's the way to bet.

BERTRAND ARTHUR, EARL RUSSELL
1872–1970   British philosopher

In America everybody is of the opinion that he has no social superiors,
since all men are equal, but he does not admit that he has no social
inferiors.

Unpopular Essays, 1950

The average man's opinions are much less foolish than they would
be if he thought for himself.

We have, in fact, two kinds of morality side by side; one which we
preach but do not practise, and another which we practise but seldom
preach.

Sceptical Essays, 1928

The infliction of cruelty with a good conscience is a delight to
moralists – that is why they invented hell.

Our great democracies still tend to think that a stupid man is more
likely to become honest than a clever man and our politicians take
advantage of this by pretending to be even more stupid than nature
made them.

New Hopes for a Changing World, 1951

It seems to be the fate of idealists to obtain what they have struggled
for in a form which destroys their ideals.

Marriage and Morals, 1929

Man is a credulous animal and must believe something. In the absence of good grounds for belief, he will be satisfied with bad ones.

Unpopular Essays, 1950

There are two motives for reading a book: one, that you enjoy it, the other than you can boast about it.

The Conquest of Happiness, 1930

There is no nonsense so arrant that it cannot be made the creed of the vast majority by adequate governmental action.

Unpopular Essays, 1950

Obscenity is what happens to shock some elderly and ignorant magistrate.

Look magazine, 1954

The fact that an opinion has been widely held is no evidence whatsoever that it is not utterly absurd. Indeed, in view of the silliness of the majority of mankind, a widespread belief is more likely to be foolish than sensible.

Marriage and Morals, 1929

People who are vigorous and brutal often find war enjoyable, provided that it is a victorious war and that there is not too much interference with rape and plunder. This is a great help in persuading people that wars are righteous.

Unpopular Essays, 1950

One should respect public opinion insofar as is necessary to avoid starvation and keep out of prison, but anything that goes beyond this is voluntary submission to an unnecessary tyranny.

The Conquest of Happiness, 1930

The fundamental defect of fathers is that they want their children to be a credit to them.

MARK RUTHERFORD (William Hale White)
1831–1913   British writer

Never say anything remarkable. It is sure to be wrong.

Last Pages from a Journal, 1915

S

MARQUIS DE SADE
1740–1814   French philosopher

All universal moral principles are idle fancies.

The 120 Days of Sodom, 1785

FRANÇOISE SAGAN
1935–   French novelist

Every little girl knows about love. It is only her capacity to suffer because of it that increases.

Daily Express, 1957

We cry when we are born, and what follows can only be an attenuation of this cry.

Ibid.

SAKI (H. H. Munro)
1870–1916   British short-story writer and journalist

Every profession has its secrets . . . if it hadn't it wouldn't be a profession.

'The Story of St. Vespaluus', 1911

I always say beauty is only sin deep.

'Reginald's Choir Treat', 1904

I think she must have been very strictly brought up, she's so desperately anxious to do the wrong thing correctly.

'Reginald on Worries', 1904

A little inaccuracy sometimes saves tons of explanation.

'The Comments of Moung Ka'

171

People may say what they like about the decay of Christianity; the religious system that produced green Chartreuse can never really die.

'Reginald on Christmas Presents', 1904

The Princess had always defended a friend's complexion if it was really bad. With her . . . charity began at homeliness and did not generally progress much further.

'Reginald in Russia', 1910

The young have aspirations that never come to pass, the old have reminiscences of what never happened.

'Reginald at the Carlton', 1904

Scandal is merely the compassionate allowance which the gay make to the humdrum.

Ibid.

All decent people live beyond their incomes nowadays, and those who aren't respectable live beyond other people's. A few gifted individuals manage to do both.

'The Match-maker', 1911

A woman who takes her husband about with her everywhere is like a cat that goes on playing with a mouse long after she's killed it.

MME DE SALM-DYCK
French writer

We like to moralise when we are old because it makes a merit of many deprivations which have become a necessity.

quoted in *A Cynic's Breviary* by J. R. Solly, 1925

CARL SANDBURG
1878–1967 American poet

Shame is the feeling you have when you agree with the woman who loves you that you are the man she thinks you are.

Incidentals

GEORGE SANDERS
1906–1972 British film star

An actor is not quite a human being – but then, who is?

Dear World, I am leaving you because I am bored. I am leaving you with your worries. Good luck.

suicide note, 1972

GEORGE SANTAYANA
1863–1952   American writer and philosopher

Few revolutionists would be such if they were heirs to a baronetcy.

Fanaticism consists in redoubling your effort when you have forgotten your aim.

The Life of Reason, 1905–6

People who feel themselves to be exiles in this world are mightily inclined to believe themselves citizens of another.

The working of great institutions is mainly the result of a vast mass of routine, petty malice, self interest, carelessness and sheer mistake. Only a residual fraction is thought.

The Crime of Galileo

Life is not a spectacle or a feast; it is a predicament.

quoted in *The Perpetual Pessimist* by Sagittarius and George

NATHALIE SARRAUTE
1902–   French academic

Television has lifted the manufacture of banality out of the sphere of handicraft and placed it in that of a major industry.

JEAN-PAUL SARTRE
1905–1980   French writer and philosopher

The poor don't know that their function in life is to exercise our generosity.

The Words, 1964

I confused things with their names; that is belief.

Ibid.

Hell is other people.

Huis clos, 1945

Human life begins on the other side of despair.

The Flies, 1943

Man is condemned to be free.

Existentialism is a Humanism

Truth and Myth are the same thing . . . you have to simulate passion to feel it, . . . man is a creature of ceremony.

The Words, 1964

'SATURDAY NIGHT AND SUNDAY MORNING'

Albert Finney: What I'm out for's a good time. All the rest is propaganda.

directed by Karel Reisz, 1960

DOROTHY L. SAYERS
1893–1957   British writer

As I grow older and older
And totter towards the tomb
I find that I care less and less
Who goes to bed with whom.

ARTHUR SCARGILL
1938–   British trades unionist

An idealist – that implies you aren't going to achieve something.

1974

FRIEDRICH VON SCHILLER
1759–1805   German playwright and poet

Whoever is foremost leads the herd.

ARTHUR SCHLESINGER, Jr.
1917–   American political advisor and academic

All wars are popular for the first thirty days.

AURÉLIEN SCHOLL
1833–1902   French aphorist

The conscience is a watch that everyone sets by the time of his own country.
> quoted in *Reflections on the Art of Life* by J. R. Solly, 1902

BUDD SCHULBERG
1914–   American writer

Living with a conscience is like driving a car with the brakes on.
> *What Makes Sammy Run*, 1941

ALBERT SCHWEITZER
1875–1965   German philosopher

Man is a clever animal who behaves like an imbecile.

HAZEL SCOTT
American feminist

Any woman who has a lot to offer the world is in trouble.
> *Ms* magazine, 1976

PETE SEEGER
1919–   American folk singer

Do you know the difference between education and experience? Education is when you read the fine print; experience is what you get when you don't.
> quoted in *Loose Talk*, ed. L. Botts, 1980

PETER SELLERS
1925–1980   British film star

People will swim through shit if you put a few bob in it.

LUCIUS ANNAEUS SENECA
c. 4 BC – AD 65   Roman philosopher and playwright

Successful and fortunate crime is called virtue.

Hercules Furens, 1st century

ERIC SEVAREID
1912–   American newscaster

The chief cause of problems is solutions.

1970

MME DE SÉVIGNÉ
1626–1696   French letter writer

The more I see of men the more I admire dogs.

GEORGE BERNARD SHAW
1856–1950   Irish playwright and critic

An Englishman does everything on principle: he fights you on patriotic principles; he robs you on business principles; he enslaves you on imperial principles.

The Man of Destiny, 1907

A pessimist is a man who thinks everybody is as nasty as himself and hates them for it.

When a stupid man is doing something he is ashamed of, he always declares that it is his duty.

Caesar and Cleopatra, 1901

Self-sacrifice enables us to sacrifice other people without blushing.

Fashions, after all, are only induced epidemics.

The Doctor's Dilemma, 1913

Self-denial is not a virtue: it is only the effect of prudence on rascality.

Man and Superman, 1903

Morality consists in suspecting other people of not being legally married.

> *The Doctor's Dilemma*, 1913

The more things a man is ashamed of, the more respectable he is.

> *Man and Superman*, 1903

A drama critic is a man who leaves no turn unstoned.

> quoted in *New York Times*, 1950

What is virtue but the trades unionism of the married?

> *Man and Superman*, 1903

First love is only a little foolishness and a lot of curiosity, no really self-respecting woman would take advantage of it.

> *John Bull's Other Island*, 1907

The art of government is the organisation of idolatry. The bureaucracy consists of functionaries; the aristocracy of idols; the democracy of idolators. The populace cannot understand the bureaucracy, it can only worship the national idols.

Assassination is the extreme form of censorship.

> *The Shewing Up of Blanco Posnet*, 1916

The nauseous sham goodfellowship our democratic public men get up for shop use.

> *Back to Methuselah*, 1921

Martyrdom is the only way in which a man can become famous without ability.

> *Fabian Essays*, 1908

It is most unwise for people in love to marry.

Revolutions have never lightened the burden of tyranny, they have only shifted it to another shoulder.

> *Man and Superman*, 1903

The fickleness of the women whom I love is only equalled by the infernal constancy of the women who love me.

> *The Philanderer*

When we want to read of the deeds that are done for love, whither do we turn? To the murder column.

The only way for a woman to provide for herself decently is for her to be good to some man that can afford to be good to her.

Mrs. Warren's Profession, 1898

The ideal love affair is conducted by post.

Democracy substitutes election by the incompetent many for appointment by the corrupt few.

Man and Superman, 1903

Liberty means responsibility, that is why most men dread it.

Ibid.

I have a technical objection to making sexual infatuation a tragic theme. Experience proves that it is only effective in the comic spirit.

Three Plays for Puritans, 1901

Alcohol is a very necessary article . . . It enables Parliament to do things at eleven at night that no sane person would do at eleven in the morning.

Major Barbara, 1907

Physically there is nothing to distinguish human society from the farm-yard except that children are more troublesome and costly than chickens and women are not so completely enslaved as farm stock.

Getting Married

SHAW'S SYSTEM

Build a system that even a fool can use, and only a fool will want to use it.

quoted in *Murphy's Law* by A. Bloch, 1979

EDGAR A. SHOAFF

Advertising is the art of making whole lies out of half truths.

quoted in *Peter's Quotations* by L. Peter, 1977

ANDRÉ SIEGFRIED
1875–1959   French writer

Do you want to injure someone's reputation? Don't speak ill of him, speak too well.

Quelques maximes, 1943

A well governed people are generally a people who do not think much.

Inédit

POSY SIMMONDS
1948– British cartoonist

'All I want is us to share the occasional candle-lit dinner and a bit of slap and tickle when your old man's away on business. No involvement. No strings. No complications.'
'Oh Myles, this is too wonderful.' Relief flooded her entire being. Here at last was the casual fling she had always dreamed of.

True Love, 1981

FRANK H. SIMONDS
1878–1936 American journalist

There is but one way for a newspaperman to look at a politician, and that is down.

FRANK SINATRA
1915– American singer and film star

Hell hath no fury like a hustler with a literary agent.

1977

RED SKELTON
1910– American film star

surveying the funeral of Hollywood mogul Harry Cohn, 1958:

It proves what they say, give the public what they want to see and they'll come out for it.

(Also attributed to Samuel Goldwyn, attending Louis B. Mayer's obsequies, 1957.)

CORNELIA OTIS SKINNER
1901–1979 American actress and writer

Woman's virtue is man's greatest invention.

PHILIP SLATER
1927– American writer

There is no such thing as a situation so intolerable that human beings must necessarily rise up against it. People can bear anything, and the longer it exists the more placidly they will bear it.

The Pursuit of Loneliness, 1970

CHARLES MERRILL SMITH
American writer

The cocktail party – a device for paying off obligations to people you don't want to invite to dinner.

Instant Status, 1972

H. ALLEN SMITH
1907–1976 American journalist

When there are two conflicting versions of the story, the wise course is to believe the one in which people appear at their worst.

Let the Crabgrass Grow, 1960

HORACE SMITH
1779–1849 British author

Good advice is one of those injuries which a good man ought, if possible, to forgive, but at all events to forget at once.

An absurdity is anything advanced by our opponents, contrary to our own practice, or above our comprehension.

quoted in *Definitive Quotations*, ed. J. Ferguson, 1981

Courage is the fear of being thought a coward.

LOGAN PEARSALL SMITH
1865–1946 American essayist

How many of our daydreams would darken into nightmares were there any danger of their coming true.

quoted in *The Faber Book of Aphorisms*,
ed. Auden and Kronenberger, 1964

The denunciation of the young is a necessary part of the hygiene of older people, and greatly assists the circulation of their blood.

Last Words, 1933

All reformers, however strict their social conscience, live in houses just as big as they can pay for.

What is more enchanting than the voices of young people when you can't hear what they say.

All Trivia

When they come downstairs from their ivory towers, idealists are apt to walk straight into the gutter.

How awful to reflect that what people say of us is true.

All Trivia

There are two things to aim at in life: first, to get what you want, and after that to enjoy it. Only the wisest of mankind achieve the second.

Afterthoughts

There are few sorrows, however poignant, in which a good income is of no avail.

Ibid.

NANCY BANKS SMITH
British journalist

In my experience, if you have to keep the lavatory door shut by extending your left leg, it's modern architecture.

Guardian, 1969

STEVIE SMITH
1902–1971   British poet

There you are you see, quite simply, if you cannot have your dear husband for a comfort and a delight, for a breadwinner and a crosspatch, for a sofa, a chair or a hotwater bottle, one can use him as a Cross to be borne.

REV. SYDNEY SMITH
1771–1845   English clergyman and wit

I have no relish for the country: it is a kind of grave.

letter, 1838

PHILIP SNOWDEN
British politician

It would be desirable if every government, when it comes to power, should have its old speeches burned.

SOLON
c. 640 – c. 558 BC   Greek law-giver

Laws are like spiders' webs which, if anything small falls into them they ensnare it, but large things break through and escape.
quoted in *Lives and Opinions of Eminent Philosophers* by D. Laertius

DUNCAN SPAETH

I know why the sun never sets on the British Empire – God wouldn't trust an Englishman in the dark.

quoted in *The Book of Insults* by N. McPhee, 1978

JOSEPH STALIN (Joseph Djugashvili)
1879–1953   Russian dictator

A single death is a tragedy, a million deaths is a statistic.

Sincere diplomacy is no more possible than dry water or wooden iron.

ROD STEIGER
1925–   American film star

That's all religion is – some principle you believe in . . . man has accomplished far more miracles than the God he invented. What a tragedy it is to invent a God and then suffer to keep him King.

Playboy magazine, 1969

JOHN STEINBECK
1902–1968   American novelist

The profession of book writing makes horse racing seem like a solid, stable business.

Newsweek magazine, 1962

DR WILHELM STEKHEL

Many an attack of depression is nothing but the expression of regret at having to be virtuous.

The Depths of the Soul

STENDHAL (Henri Beyle)
1783–1842   French novelist

All religions are founded on the fear of the many and the cleverness of the few.

The only excuse for God is that he doesn't exist.

JUDITH STERN

Experience – a comb life gives you after you lose your hair.

ADLAI STEVENSON
1900–1965   American politician

A lie is an abomination unto the Lord and a very present help in trouble.

1951

An editor is one who separates the wheat from the chaff and prints the chaff.

In America any boy may become President, and I suppose that's just the risk he takes.

1952

ROBERT LOUIS STEVENSON
1850–1894   British writer

If we take matrimony at its lowest . . . if we regard it as no more than a sort of friendship recognised by the police.

Virginibus Puerisque, 1881

GENERAL 'VINEGAR JOE' STILWELL
American soldier

The higher a monkey climbs, the more you can see of his behind.

CASKIE STINNETT
1911–   American writer

A diplomat is a person who can tell you to go to hell in such a way that you actually look forward to the trip.

Out of the Red, 1960

MAX STIRNER
1806–1856   German writer

The state calls its own violence law, but that of the individual crime.

BARONESS STOCKS
1895–1975   British writer

We don't call it sin today, we call it self-expression.

I. F. STONE
1907–   American journalist

Every government is run by liars and nothing they say should be believed.

Every government is a device by which a few control the actions of many . . . on both sides at the moment complex human societies depend for the final decisions of war and peace on a group of elderly men any sensible plant personnel manager, whether under capitalism or Communism, would hesitate to hire.

1959

The two party system . . . is a triumph of the dialectic. It showed that two could be one and one could be two and had probably been fabricated by Hegel for the American market on a subcontract from General Dynamics.

> 1968

Those who set out nobly to be their brother's keeper sometimes end up by becoming his jailer. Every emancipation has in it the seeds of a new slavery, and every truth easily becomes a lie.

> 1969

The important thing about the so-called 'communications industry' is that it is basically concerned with merchandising. News is a kind of by-product and if you want to sell things, you don't want to offend anybody.

> *The Listener*, 1963

TOM STOPPARD
1937– British playwright

It's better to be quotable than to be honest.

> *Guardian*, 1973

Life is a gamble at terrible odds, if it was a bet you wouldn't take it.

> *Rosencrantz and Guildenstern Are Dead*, 1967

LIONEL STRACHEY
1864–1927

To be patriotic, hate all nations but your own; to be religious, all sects but your own; to be moral, all pretences but your own.

AUGUST STRINDBERG
1849–1912   Swedish playwright

The Family! Home of all social evils, a charitable institution for indolent women, a prison workshop for the slaving breadwinner and a hell for children.

> *The Son of a Servant*, 1886

Sacred family! . . . The supposed home of all the virtues, where innocent children are tortured into their first falsehoods, where wills are broken by parental tyranny, and self-respect smothered by crowded, jostling egos.

Ibid.

SIR JOHN SUCKLING
1609–1642   British poet

Out upon it, I have loved
Three whole days together
And am like to love three more
If it prove fair weather.

'Fragmenta Aurea', 1646

'SUDDENLY LAST SUMMER'

Elizabeth Taylor: Is that what love is? Using people? And maybe that's what hate is. Not being able to use people.

screenplay by Gore Vidal and Tennessee Williams, 1959

DR EDITH SUMMERSKILL
1901–   British politician

Nagging is the repetition of unpalatable truths.

Observer, 1960

JONATHAN SWIFT
1667–1745   British satirist, poet and essayist

There is nothing in this world constant but inconstancy.

A Critical Essay upon the Faculties of Mind, 1707

Party is the madness of many for the gain of a few.
(cf. Pope)

Thoughts on Various Subjects, 1711

Happiness is the perpetual possession of being well deceived.

When a true genius appears in the world you may know him by this sign: that all the dunces are in confederacy against him.

When men grow virtuous in their old age, they only make a sacrifice to God of the devil's leavings.

Satire is a sort of glass, wherein beholders do generally discover everybody's face but their own.

The Battle of the Books, 1704

Promises and pie-crust are made to be broken.

A Complete Collection of Polite and Ingenious Conversation, 1738

THOMAS SZASZ
1920– American psychoanalyst

If you talk to God, you are praying; if God talks to you, you have schizophrenia.

The Second Sin

Two wrongs don't make a right, but they make a good excuse.

Ibid.

Happiness is an imaginary condition, formerly attributed by the living to the dead, now usually attributed by adults to children, and by children to adults.

Ibid.

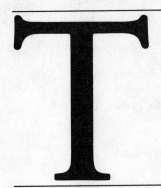

HIPPOLYTE TAINE
1828–1893   French philosopher, critic and historian

We study ourselves three weeks, we love each other three months, we squabble three years, we tolerate each other thirty years, and then the children start all over again.

Vie et opinions de Thomas Graingorge

CHARLES-MAURICE DE TALLEYRAND
1754–1838   French statesman

Never speak ill of yourself, your friends will always say enough on that subject.

quoted in *A Cynic's Breviary* by J. R. Solly, 1925

Speech was given to man to conceal his thoughts.

quoted in *Reflections on the Art of Life* by J. R. Solly, 1902

R. H. TAWNEY
1880–1962   British historian

Governments, like individuals, should beware when all men speak well of them.

Guardian, 1963

SIR HENRY TAYLOR
1800–1886   British playwright

Conscience is, in most men, an anticipation of the opinions of others.

TERRY-THOMAS
1911–   British comedian

Do not assume that the other fellow has intelligence to match yours.
He may have more.

MARGARET THATCHER
1925–   British Prime Minister

No-one would remember the Good Samaritan if he had only had good
intentions. He had money as well.

quoted in the *Spectator*, 1980

You don't tell deliberate lies, but sometimes you have to be evasive.

1976

THEOPHRASTUS
c. 370 – 287 BC   Greek philosopher

Love is the affection of a mind that has nothing better to engage it.

'THE THIRD MAN'

Orson Welles: In Switzerland they had brotherly love, five hundred
years of democracy and peace and what did they produce? The
cuckoo clock!

screenplay by Graham Greene and Orson Welles, 1949

DYLAN THOMAS
1914–1953   British poet

An alcoholic is someone you don't like who drinks as much as you
do.

HUNTER S. THOMPSON
1939–   American journalist

America . . . just a nation of two hundred million used car salesmen
with all the money we need to buy guns and no qualms about killing
anybody else in the world who tries to make us uncomfortable.

Fear and Loathing on the Campaign Trail, 1972

HENRY DAVID THOREAU
1817–1862   American essayist and poet

What men call social virtues, good fellowship, is commonly but the virtue of pigs in a litter, which lie close together to keep each other warm.

Journal, 1851

We should distrust any enterprise that requires new clothes.

That government is best which governs least.

Civil Disobedience, 1849

What is commonly called friendship is only a little more honour among rogues.

JAMES THURBER
1894–1964   American humorist

A man should not insult his wife publicly, at parties. He should insult her in the privacy of the home.

Thurber Country, 1953

Let the meek inherit the earth – they have it coming to them.

Life magazine, 1960

HENRIETTA TIARKS
1940–   British socialite

A gentleman is a patient wolf.

1957

LEO TOLSTOY
1828–1910   Russian novelist

Women are well aware that what is commonly called sublime and poetical love depends not upon moral qualities, but on frequent meetings, and on the style in which the hair is done up, and on the colour and the cut of the dress.

The Kreutzer Sonata, 1890

History is nothing but a collection of fables and useless trifles, cluttered up with a mass of unnecessary figures and proper names.

1846

NICOLAS TOMALIN
d. 1973   British journalist

The only qualities for real success in journalism are ratlike cunning, a plausible manner and a little literary ability. The capacity to steal other people's ideas and phrases . . . is also invaluable.

Stop the Press, I Want to Get On

LILY TOMLIN
1939–   American comedienne

The trouble with the rat-race is that even if you win, you're still a rat.

HORNE TOOKE
1736–1812   British radical

If you would be powerful, pretend to be powerful.

ACHILLE TOURNIER
19th century French aphorist

Man persuades himself he is emancipated every time he decorates a new servitude with the name of liberty.

quoted in *The Oxford Book of Aphorisms*, ed. J. Gross, 1983

When one knows women one pities men, but when one studies men, one excuses women.

quoted in *A Cynic's Breviary* by J. R. Solly, 1925

LIONEL TRILLING
1905–1975   American critic

Immature artists imitate, mature artists steal.

Esquire magazine, 1962

We who are liberal and progressive know that the poor are our equals in every sense except that of being equal to us.

The Liberal Imagination, 1950

ELSA TRIOLET
1896–1970   French writer

To be a prophet it is sufficient to be a pessimist.

Elsa's Proverbs

HARRY S. TRUMAN
1884–1972   American President

A leader is a man who has the ability to get other people to do what they don't want to do and like it.

It's a recession when your neighbour loses his job; it's a depression when you lose yours.

1958

If you can't convince them, confuse them.

A politician is a man who understands government and it takes a politician to run a government. A statesman is a politician who's been dead ten or fifteen years.

1958

MARINA TSVETAYEVA
b. 1892   Russian poet

Freedom – a drunken whore
Sprawling in a power maddened soldier's arms.

BARBARA TUCHMAN
1912–   American historian

War is the unfolding of miscalculations.

The Guns of August, 1962

SOPHIE TUCKER
1884–1966   American singer

From birth to age eighteen a girl needs good parents, from eighteen to thirty-five she needs good looks, from thirty-five she needs a good personality. From fifty-five on, she needs good cash.

1953

JEREMY TUNSTALL
1934– British writer

It has been said that Public Relations is the art of wining friends and getting people under the influence.

The Advertising Man, 1964

E. S. TURNER
1909– British writer

Advertising is the whip which hustles humanity up the road to the Better Mousetrap. It is the vision which reproaches man for the paucity of his desires.

The Shocking History of Advertising, 1952

LANA TURNER
1920– American film star

A successful man is one who makes more money than his wife can spend. A successful woman is one who can find such a man.

1980

MARK TWAIN (Samuel Clemens)
1835–1910 American humorist

A classic is something that everyone wants to have read and nobody wants to read.

The Disappearance of Literature, 1900

The radical invents the views. When he has worn them out, the conservative adopts them.

Notebooks, 1935

Few things are harder to put up with than the annoyance of a good example.

Good breeding consists in concealing how much we think of ourselves and how little we think of the other person.

If you pick up a starving dog and make him prosperous, he will not bite you; that is the principal difference between a dog and a man.

If man had created man, he would be ashamed of his performance.

Notebooks, 1935

Talking of patriotism, what humbug it is; it is a word which always commemorates a robbery. There isn't a foot of land in the world which doesn't represent the ousting and re-ousting of a long line of successive owners.

A Connecticut Yankee at King Arthur's Court, 1889

Nothing so needs reforming as other people's habits.

1894

In statesmanship get the formalities right, never mind about the moralities.

The world consists of the dangerously insane and such that are not.

Notebooks, 1935

KENNETH TYNAN
1927–1980   British film and theatre critic

Show me a congenital eavesdropper with the instincts of a Peeping Tom and I will show you the makings of a dramatist.

Pausing on the Stairs, 1957

A critic is a man who knows the way but can't drive the car.

New York Times, 1966

A good many inconveniences attend play-going in any large city, but the greatest of them is usually the play itself.

New York Herald Tribune, 1957

The liberal [on pornography] . . . is like a man who loathes whorehouses in practice, but doesn't mind them in principle, providing they are designed by Mies van der Rohe and staffed by social workers in Balenciaga dresses.

Esquire magazine, 1968

PETER USTINOV
1921– British actor and wit

That weakness in human nature which goes by the name of strength.
The Listener, 1974

Glamour in the theatre is usually twenty chorus girls in a line all doing the same thing. It is assumed that twenty women are more glamorous than one.
Time and Tide magazine

The habit of religion is oppressive, an easy way out of thought.
Everybody's magazine, 1957

An optimist is one who knows exactly how bad a place the world can be; a pessimist is one who finds out anew every morning.
Illustrated London News, 1968

British education is probably the best in the world, if you can survive it. If you can't there is nothing left for you but the diplomatic corps.
Time and Tide magazine

PAUL VALÉRY
1871–1956   French poet and critic

God created man, and finding him not sufficiently alone, gave him a companion to make him feel his solitude more.

Tel quel, 1943

A man who is 'of sound mind' is one who keeps the inner madman under lock and key.

Mauvaises pensées et autres, 1942

Politics is the art of preventing people from taking part in affairs which properly concern them.

Tel quel, 1943

ABIGAIL VAN BUREN
1918–   American agony columnist

People who fight fire with fire usually end up with ashes.

1974

GUSTAVE VAPEREAU
French aphorist

Women are always anxious to urge bachelors to matrimony; is it from charity, or revenge?

quoted in *A Cynic's Breviary* by J. R. Solly, 1925

V

MARQUIS DE VAUVENARGUES
1715–1747 French moralist

There are many things we despise in order that we may not have to despise ourselves.

Reflections and Maxims, 1746

BILL VEECK
1914– American sports entrepreneur

The only promotion rules I can think of are that a sense of shame is to be avoided at all costs and there is never any reason for a hustler to be less cunning than more virtuous men. Oh yes . . . whenever you think you've got something really great, add ten per cent more.

1965

A hustler is a man who will talk you into giving him a free ride and make it seem as if he is doing you a great favour.

1965

GORE VIDAL
1925– American novelist and critic

To the right wing 'law and order' is often just a code phrase, meaning 'get the niggers'. To the left wing it often means political oppression.

1975

Sex is. There is nothing more to be done about it. Sex builds no roads, writes no novels and sex certainly gives no meaning to anything in life but itself.

'Norman Mailer's Self-Advertisements', 1960

The genius of our ruling class is that it has kept a majority of the people from ever questioning the inequity of a system where most people drudge along paying heavy taxes for which they get nothing in return.

Having no talent is no longer enough.

Wisdom is deepest platitude.

on London Weekend Television, 1981

'After she was dead, I loved her.' That is the story of every life – and death.

New York Review of Books, 1980

I can understand companionship. I can understand bought sex in the afternoon. I cannot understand the love affair.

Sunday Times, 1973

The man and woman make love, attain climax, fall separate. Then she whispers 'I'll tell you who I was thinking of if you tell me who you were thinking of.' Like most sex jokes the origins of the pleasant exchange are obscure. But whatever the source, it seldom fails to evoke a certain awful recognition.

New York Review of Books, 1966

The hatred Americans have for their own government is pathological ... at one level it is simply thwarted greed: since our religion is making a buck, giving a part of that buck to any government is an act against nature.

On the whole history tends to be rather poor fiction – except at its best.

Writers at Work, 4th series, 1981

What is there to say, finally, except that pain is bad and pleasure good, life all, death nothing.

Esquire magazine, 1970

For certain people, after fifty, litigation takes the place of sex.

Evening Standard, 1981

A. VINET
French writer

When a benefactor has no other confidant than the beneficiary, his secret, as a rule, is only too safe.

quoted in *A Cynic's Breviary* by J. R. Solly, 1925

VO DONG GIANG
Vietnamese politician

Do not fear when your enemies criticise you. Beware when they applaud.

Time magazine, 1978

VOLTAIRE (François Marie Arouet)
1694–1778   French satirist, philosopher and writer

Animals have these advantages over man: they have no theologians to instruct them, their funerals cost them nothing, and no-one starts law suits over their wills.

As a rule men are foolish, ungrateful, jealous, covetous of others' goods, abusing their superiority when they are strong and rascals when they are weak.

quoted in *A Cynic's Breviary* by J. R. Solly, 1925

To announce truths, to propose something useful to mankind, is an infallible receipt for being persecuted.

Ibid.

It is dangerous to be right in matters on which the established authorities are wrong.

Ibid.

Marriage is the only adventure open to the cowardly.

Thoughts of a Philosopher

Originality is nothing but judicious imitation.

We use ideas merely to justify our evil, and speech merely to conceal our ideas.

Dialogue XIV

When he who hears doesn't understand him who speaks, and when he who speaks doesn't know what he himself means – that is philosophy.

Candide, 1759

In general, the art of government consists in taking as much money as possible from one party of the citizens to give to the other.

To succeed in chaining the multitude you must seem to wear the same fetters.

> *Philosophical Dictionary*, 1764

Divorce is probably of nearly the same date as marriage. I believe, however, that marriage is some weeks the more ancient.

> *Ibid.*

The pleasure of governing must certainly be exquisite, if we may judge from the vast numbers who are eager to be concerned with it.

> *Ibid.*

The world is a vast temple dedicated to Discord.

> letter, 1752

Men will always be mad, and those who think they can cure them are the maddest of all.

> letter, 1762

The art of medicine consists in amusing the patient while nature cures the disease.

A clergyman is one who feels himself called upon to live without working at the expense of the rascals who work to live.

If God did not exist, it would be necessary to invent him.

> *Épîtres*, XCVI

Illusion is the first of the pleasures.

In the great game of human life one begins by being a dupe and ends by being a rogue.

All our history . . . is no more than accepted fiction.

> *Jeannot et Colin*

Once the people begin to reason, all is lost.

> letter, 1766

KURT VONNEGUT, Jr.
1922– American writer

It strikes me as gruesome and comical that in our culture we have an expectation that a man can always solve his problems. This is so untrue that it makes me want to cry – or laugh.

> *Playboy* magazine, 1973

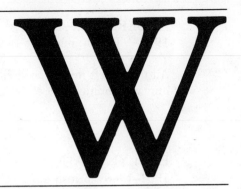

JAMES J. WALKER
1881–1946   American politician

A reformer is a man who rides through a sewer in a glass-bottomed boat.

EDGAR WALLACE
1875–1932   British novelist

What is a highbrow? It is a man who has found something more interesting than women.

interviewed, 1931

ANDY WARHOL
1926–   American artist

What we're all looking for is someone who doesn't live there, just pays for it.

From A to B and Back Again, 1975

WARREN'S RULE

To spot the expert, pick the one who predicts the job will take the longest and cost the most.

quoted in *Murphy's Law Book Two* by A. Bloch, 1980

GEORGE WASHINGTON
1732–1799   American President

Whenever one person is found adequate to the discharge of a duty by close application thereto, it is worse executed by two persons and scarcely done at all if three or more are employed therein.

201

AUBERON WAUGH
1939– British journalist

All that is left for the civilised man is to laugh at the absurdity of the human condition.

Esquire magazine, 1968

EVELYN WAUGH
1903–1966 British novelist

Aesthetic value is often the by-product of the artist striving to do something else.

The Letters of Evelyn Waugh, ed. Mark Amory, 1980

Manners are especially the need of the plain. The pretty can get away with anything.

Observer, 1962

Mr. Salter's side of the conversation was limited to expressions of assent. When Lord Copper was right he said 'Definitely, Lord Copper'; when he was wrong, 'Up to a point.'
'Let me see, what's the name of the place I mean? Capital of Japan? Yokohama isn't it?'
'Up to a point, Lord Copper.'
'And Hong Kong definitely belongs to us, doesn't it?'
'Definitely, Lord Copper.'

Scoop, 1938

SIMONE WEIL
1909–1943 French philosopher

Culture is an instrument wielded by professors to manufacture professors, who when their turn comes, will manufacture professors.

The Need for Roots, 1952

A. H. WEILER
Nothing is impossible for the man who doesn't have to do it himself.

New York Times, 1968

ORSON WELLES
1915– American film director

When you are down and out something always turns up – and it is usually the noses of your friends.

New York Times, 1962

THE DUKE OF WELLINGTON
1769–1852 British soldier and Prime Minister

There are no manifestos like cannon and musketry.

CAROLYN WELLS
187?–1942 American writer

A guilty conscience is the mother of invention.

H. G. WELLS
1866–1946 British writer

Moral indignation is jealousy with a halo.

Human history becomes more and more a race between education and catastrophe.

The Outline of History, 1921

MAE WEST
1892–1980 American film star

When choosing between two evils, I always like to take the one I've never tried before.

in Klondike Annie, 1936

Give a man a free hand and he'll run it all over you.

Keep a diary and one day it'll keep you.

REBECCA WEST (Cicily Fairfield)
1892–1983   British writer

Just how difficult it is to write biography can be reckoned by anybody who sits down and considers just how many people know the real truth about his or her love affairs.

Vogue magazine, 1952

GENERAL WILLIAM WESTMORELAND
1914–   American soldier

Command is getting people to go the way you want them to go – enthusiastically.

RUTH WESTON
American actress

A fox is a wolf who sends flowers.

1955

E. B. WHITE
1899–   American essayist and humorist

The trouble with the profit system has always been that it was highly unprofitable to most people.

One Man's Meat, 1944

EDMUND WHITE
1940–   American writer

Someone once remarked that in adolescence pornography is a substitute for sex, whereas in adulthood sex is a substitute for pornography.

New Times magazine, 1979

ALFRED NORTH WHITEHEAD
1861–1947   British philosopher

The major advances in civilisation are processes that all but wreck the societies in which they occur.

'Necessity is the mother of invention' is a silly proverb. 'Necessity is the mother of futile dodges' is much nearer the truth.
>> quoted in *The Faber Book of Aphorisms*,
>> ed. Auden and Kronenberger, 1964

Morality . . . is what the majority then and there happen to like and immorality . . . is what they dislike.

KATHERINE WHITEHORN
British journalist

In heaven they will bore you, in hell you will bore them.

An office party is not, as is sometimes supposed, the Managing Director's chance to kiss the tea-girl. It is the tea-girl's chance to kiss the Managing Director (however bizarre an ambition this may seem to anyone who has seen the Managing Director face on).
>> *Roundabout*

The best careers advice to give to the young is 'Find out what you like doing best and get someone to pay you for doing it.'
>> *Observer*, 1975

CEDRIC WHITMAN
1916– American classicist

Mythology is what grownups believe, folklore is what they tell children and religion is both.
>> 1969

CHARLOTTE WHITTON
1896–1975

Whatever women do they must do twice as well as men to be thought half as good. Luckily this is not difficult.
>> quoted in *The Book of Insults* by N. McPhee, 1978

NORBERT WIENER
1894–1964 American mathematician

A conscience which has been bought once will be bought twice.
>> *The Human Use of Human Beings*, 1954

OSCAR WILDE
1854–1900   Irish playwright, poet and wit

A thing is not necessarily true because a man dies for it.
The Portrait of Mr. W.H.

I sometimes think that God, in creating man, somewhat overestimated his ability.

In America the President rules for four years and journalism governs for ever and ever.

High hopes were once formed of democracy, but democracy means simply the bludgeoning of the people, by the people, for the people.
The Soul of Man under Socialism, 1891

There is much to be said in favour of modern journalism. By giving us the opinions of the uneducated, it keeps us in touch with the ignorance of the community.
The Critic as Artist, 1891

The history of women is the history of the worst tyranny the world has ever known: the tyranny of the weak over the strong. It is the only tyranny that ever lasts.
A Woman of No Importance, 1894

Romance should never begin with sentiment. It should begin with science and end with a settlement.
An Ideal Husband, 1899

A man who moralises is usually a hypocrite and a woman who moralises is invariably plain.
Lady Windermere's Fan, 1893

One should always be in love. That is the reason why one should never marry.

Philanthropy seems to me to have become simply the refuge of people who want to annoy their fellow creatures.
An Ideal Husband, 1899

The only thing that consoles man for the stupid things he does is the praise he always gives himself for doing them.

What people call insincerity is simply a method by which we can multiply our personalities.
The Critic as Artist, 1890

To be natural is such a very difficult pose to keep up.
An Ideal Husband, 1899

He has nothing. He looks everything. What more can one desire?
The Importance of Being Earnest, 1899

Education is an admirable thing, but it is well to remember from time to time that nothing that is worth knowing can be taught.
The Critic as Artist, 1890

Relations are simply a tedious pack of people, who haven't the remotest knowledge of how to live, nor the smallest instinct about when to die.
The Importance of Being Earnest, 1899

To get back one's youth one has merely to repeat one's follies.
The Picture of Dorian Gray, 1891

Morality is simply the attitude we adopt to people whom we personally dislike.
An Ideal Husband, 1899

The truth is rarely pure and never simple. Modern life would be very tedious if it were either, and modern literature a complete impossibility.
The Importance of Being Earnest, 1899

If one tells the truth, one is sure, sooner or later, to be found out.
Phrases and Philosophies for the Use of the Young, 1894

To be good, according to the vulgar standard of goodness, is obviously quite easy. It merely requires a certain amount of sordid terror, a certain lack of imaginative thought, and a certain low passion for middle-class respectability.
The Critic as Artist, 1890

Rich bachelors should be heavily taxed. It is not fair that some men should be happier than others.

When one is in love one begins by deceiving oneself. And one ends by deceiving others. This is what the world calls a romance.
A Woman of No Importance, 1893

The one charm of marriage is that it makes a life of deception absolutely necessary for both parties.
The Picture of Dorian Gray, 1891

There is nothing in the world like the devotion of a married woman.
It's a thing no married man knows anything about.

Lady Windermere's Fan, 1893

Most people are other people. Their thoughts are someone else's
opinions, their lives a mimicry, their passions a quotation.

De Profundis, 1905

Good resolutions are useless attempts to interfere with scientific laws.
Their origin is pure vanity. Their result is absolutely nil. They give us,
now and then, some of those luxurious sterile emotions that have a
certain charm for the weak . . . They are simply cheques that men draw
on a bank where they have no account.

The Picture of Dorian Gray, 1891

I never came across anyone in whom the moral sense was dominant
who was not heartless, cruel, vindictive, log-stupid and entirely lacking
in the smallest sense of humanity. Moral people, as they are termed, are
simply beasts. I would sooner have fifty unnatural vices than one
unnatural virtue.

Always! that is a dreadful word . . . it is a meaningless word too. The
only difference between a caprice and a life-long passion is that the
caprice lasts a little longer.

The Picture of Dorian Gray, 1891

It is absurd to divide people into good and bad. People are either
charming or tedious.

Lady Windermere's Fan, 1893

Young people, nowadays, imagine that money is everything, and
when they grow older, they know it.

The Picture of Dorian Gray, 1891

One knows so well the popular idea of health. The English country
gentleman galloping after a fox. The unspeakable in full pursuit of the
uneatable.

A Woman of No Importance, 1894

I always pass on good advice. It is the only thing to do with it. It is
never any good to oneself.

An Ideal Husband, 1899

Murder is always a mistake – one should never do anything one
cannot talk about after dinner.

The Picture of Dorian Gray, 1891

There is only one thing in the world worse than being talked about and that is not being talked about.

Ibid.

Life is much too important a thing to talk seriously about it.

Vera, or the Nihilists, 1880

It is only an auctioneer who can equally and impartially admire all schools of art.

The Critic as Artist, 1890

People who want to say merely what is sensible should say it to themselves before they come down to breakfast in the morning, never after.

If we men married the women we deserve, we should have a very bad time of it.

An Ideal Husband, 1899

Patriotism is the virtue of the vicious.

The public have an insatiable curiosity to know everything. Except what is worth knowing. Journalism, conscious of this, and having tradesman-like habits, supplies their demands.

The Soul of Man under Socialism, 1891

All ways end at the same point . . . Disillusion.

The Picture of Dorian Gray, 1891

There is a good deal to be said for blushing, if one can do it at the proper moment.

A Woman of No Importance, 1894

Any preoccupation with ideas of what is right and wrong in conduct shows an arrested intellectual development.

Phrases and Philosophies for the Use of the Young, 1894

Religion is the fashionable substitute for belief.

The Picture of Dorian Gray, 1891

Fathers should neither be seen nor heard. That is the only proper basis for family life.

An Ideal Husband, 1899

The only duty we owe history is to rewrite it.

The Critic as Artist, 1890

Every great man nowadays has his disciples, and it is always Judas who writes the biography.

Ibid.

Only the shallow know themselves.

Phrases and Philosophies for the Use of the Young, 1894

Wickedness is a myth invented by good people to account for the curious attractiveness of others.

Ibid.

Experience is the name everyone gives to their mistakes.

Lady Windermere's Fan, 1893

Children begin by loving their parents. After a time they judge them . . . rarely, if ever, do they forgive them.

A Woman of No Importance, 1894

The basis of literary friendship is mixing the poisoned bowl.

A sentimentalist is simply one who desires to have the luxury of an emotion without paying for it.

Conscience and cowardice are really the same things. Conscience is the trade-name of the firm.

The Picture of Dorian Gray, 1891

When the gods wish to punish us they answer our prayers.

An Ideal Husband, 1899

As long as war is regarded as wicked it will always have its fascination. When it is looked upon as vulgar, it will cease to be popular.

Intentions, 1891

I always choose my friends for their good looks and my enemies for their good intellects. Man cannot be too careful in his choice of enemies.

The Picture of Dorian Gray, 1891

BILLY WILDER
1906– Austrian-American film director

Hindsight is always 20:20.

THORNTON WILDER
1897–   American novelist and playwright

Literature is the orchestration of platitudes.

Time magazine, 1953

MICHAEL WILDING
1912–1979   British actor

You can pick out the actors by the glazed look that comes into their eyes when the conversation wanders away from themselves.

JOHN WILKES
1727–1797   British radical

Life can then little else supply
But a few good fucks and then we die.

1763

KENNETH WILLIAMS
1926–   British comedian

The nicest thing about quotes is that they give us a nodding acquaintance with the originator which is often socially impressive.

Acid Drops, 1980

TENNESSEE WILLIAMS (Thomas Lanier Williams)
1914–1983   American playwright

We're all of us sentenced to solitary confinement inside our own skins, for life.

Orpheus Descending, 1957

Don't look forward to the day when you stop suffering. Because when it comes you'll know that you're dead.

Observer, 1958

We have to distrust each other. It's our only defence against betrayal.

Camino Real, 1953

GARY WILLS
1934– American writer and journalist

Only the winners decide what were war crimes.

New York Times, 1975

CHARLES E. WILSON
1890–1961 American government official

An expert is a mechanic away from home.

EARL WILSON
1907– American newspaper columnist

If you look like your passport photo, in all probability you need the journey.

Ladies' Home Journal, 1961

WOODROW WILSON
1856–1924 American President

That a peasant may become king does not render the kingdom democratic.

1917

P. G. WODEHOUSE
1881–1975 British humorist

There is only one cure for grey hair. It was invented by a Frenchman. It is called the guillotine.

The Old Reliable, 1951

Judges, as a class, display, in the matter of arranging alimony, that reckless generosity which is found only in men who are giving away someone else's cash.

Louder and Funnier, 1932

Every author really wants to have letters printed in the papers. Unable to make the grade, he drops down a rung on the ladder and writes novels.

Ibid.

CHARLES WOLF, Jr.
American writer

Those who don't study the past will repeat its errors; those who do study it will find other ways to err.

quoted in the Wall Street Journal, 1976

TOM WOLFE
1931– American writer

A cult is a religion with no political power.

In Our Time, 1980

ALEXANDER WOOLCOTT
1887–1943 American critic and writer

to a visitor during his last illness:

I have no need of your God-damned sympathy. I only wish to be entertained by some of your grosser reminiscences.

WILLIAM WORDSWORTH
1770–1850 British poet

No perverseness equals that which is supported by system, no errors are as difficult to root out as those which the understanding has pledged its credit to uphold.

Poems, 1815

SIR HENRY WOTTON
1578–1639 British diplomat

An ambassador is a honest man sent abroad to lie for the commonwealth.

1604

FRANK LLOYD WRIGHT
1869–1959 American architect

A doctor can bury his mistakes, but an architect can only advise his client to plant vines.

An expert is a man who has stopped thinking. Why should he think? He is an expert.

quoted in the Daily Express, 1959

WILLIAM WRIGLEY, Jr.
American businesman

When two men in a business always agree, one of them is unnecessary.

WOODROW WYATT
1918– British politician

Politicians who wish to succeed must be prepared to dissemble, at times to lie. All deceit is bad. In politics some deceit or moral dishonesty is the oil without which the machinery would not work.

Sunday Times, 1973

PHILIP WYLIE
1902– American writer

The first star a child gets in school for the mere performance of a needful task is its first lesson in graft.

Generation of Vipers, 1942

DOUGLAS YATES
British scientist

No scientific theory achieves public acceptance until it has been thoroughly discredited.

YIDDISH PROVERBS

If God lived on earth, people would break his windows.

The girl who can't dance says the band can't play.

When the prick stands, the brains get buried in the ground.

PETER YORK
1950– British journalist

If beauty isn't genius it usually signals at least a high level of animal cunning.

London Collection magazine, 1978

ANDREW YOUNG
1932– American politician

Nothing is illegal if one hundred businessmen decide to do it.

1976

ISRAEL ZANGWILL
1864–1926   British writer

The only true love is love at first sight; second sight dispels it.

FRANK ZAPPA
1940–   American rock musician

In the fight between you and the world, back the world.

Most rock journalism is people who can't write interviewing people who can't talk for people who can't read.

Anonymous

What men usually ask of God when they pray is that two and two not make four.

> quoted in *The Faber Book of Aphorisms*,
> ed. Auden and Kronenberger, 1964

You must not love animals, they don't last long enough. You must not love humans, they last too long.

> quoted in *A Cynic's Breviary* by J. R. Solly, 1925

Women never refer to their age until it would be wiser to ignore it.

> quoted in *Thesaurus of Epigrams*, ed. E. Fuller, 1943

Obscenity is whatever gives a judge an erection.

> American lawyer

Of course a platonic relationship is possible – but only between husband and wife.

> *Ladies' Home Journal*

The average girl would rather have beauty than brains because she knows the average man can see much better than he can think.

> quoted in *ibid.*, 1947

Don't assume that every sad-eyed woman has loved and lost – she may have got him.

Bigamy is having one husband too many, monogamy is the same.

> quoted as epigraph to *Fear of Flying* by E. Jong, 1975

The glances over cocktails
That seemed to be so sweet
Don't seem quite so amorous
Over Shredded Wheat.

> quoted in *Frank Muir Goes Into* by F. Muir, 1978

Beat your son every day; you may not know why, but he will.

Be frank and explicit with your lawyer . . . it is his business to confuse the issue afterwards.

> quoted in *A Cynic's Breviary* by J. R. Solly, 1925

Virtue, among other definitions, may thus be defined: an action against the will.

> *Characters and Observations*, early 18th century

When the client moans and sighs
Make his logo twice the size.
If he still should prove refractory,
Show a picture of his factory.
Only in the gravest cases
Should you show the clients' faces.

> Advertising agency jingle quoted in *Ogilvy on Advertising* by D. Ogilvy, 1983

You should make a point of trying every experience once – except incest and folk-dancing.

> A Scot quoted in *Farewell My Youth* by A. Bax, 1843

Marriage is an attempt to change a night owl into a homing pigeon.

> quoted in *The Penguin Book of Modern Quotations*, ed. Cohen and Cohen, 1981

There's no fun in medicine, but there's a lot of medicine in fun.

> quoted in *The Wit of Medicine*, ed. L. and M. Cowan, 1972

Faith is that quality which enables us to believe what we know to be untrue.

> quoted in *Definitive Quotations*, ed. J. Ferguson, 1981

American military censor on the ideal use of the media in war:

I wouldn't tell the people anything until the war is over, and then I'd tell them who won.

A father is a banker provided by nature.

> quoted in *The Oxford Book of Aphorisms*, ed. J. Gross, 1983

Television is summer stock in an iron lung.

> quoted in the *Manchester Guardian*, 1959

Living well is the best revenge.
(Most notably used by Robert McCallum as the title for a biography
of Gerald and Sara Murphy.)

It's what the guests say as they swing out of the drive that counts.
                                    quoted in the *New York Times*, 1947

There is one woman whom fate has destined for each of us. If we
miss her we are saved.
                                    quoted in *ibid.*, 1948

A drug is a substance that when injected into a guinea pig produces
a scientific paper.
                    quoted in *The Wit of Medicine*, ed. L. and M. Cowan, 1972

Marriage is the price men pay for sex, sex is the price woman pay
for marriage.

To our sweethearts and wives. May they never meet.
                                    19th century toast

Television – the bland leading the bland.
            quoted in *The Filmgoer's Book of Quotes*, ed. L. Halliwell, 1973

Marriage is a romance in which the hero dies in the first chapter.

He that has nothing but merit to support him is in a fair way to starve.
                        Characters and Observations, early 18th century

Adolescence: a stage between infancy and adultery.
                quoted in *H. L. Mencken's Dictionary of Quotations*, 1942

A wife is one who stands by a man in all the trouble he wouldn't
have had if he hadn't married her.

A woman needs a man like a fish needs a bicycle.
                                    Feminist slogan, 1970s

If you catch a man, throw him back.
                            Women's Liberation slogan, *c.* 1975

All husbands are alike, but they have different faces so you can tell
them apart.
                quoted in *Cassell's Book of Humorous Quotations*, 1968

A good terminology is half the game.

quoted in Bricks to Babel by A. Koestler, 1981

A husband is simply a lover with two days' growth of beard, his collar off and a bad cold in the head.

quoted in Cassell's Book of Humorous Quotations, 1968

Television is a whore. Any man who wants her full favours can have them in five minutes with a pistol.

Hijacker, quoted in Esquire magazine, 1977